Sunshine
for the
Latter-day
Saint
Missionary
Soul

Sunshine
for the
Latter-day
Saint
Missionary
Soul

EAGLE GATE

SALT LAKE CITY, UTAH

Library of Congress Cataloging-in-Publication Data

Sunshine for the Latter-day Saint missionary soul.
    p.   cm.
  ISBN 1-57345-779-5 (pbk.)
    1. Mormon missionaries—Religious life. 2. Church of Jesus Christ of Latter-day Saints—Missions.

BX8661 .S86 2000
248.4'89332—dc21

00-034794

CIP

Printed in the United States of America

54459-6669

10 9 8 7 6 5 4 3 2 1

Contents

$\mathscr{P}$reface

In the favorite Latter-day Saint hymn "Hark, All Ye Nations!" Louis F. Mönch describes those who had waited anxiously for the dawning of the restored gospel: "Searching in darkness, nations have wept; / Watching for dawn, their vigil they've kept." The cold night of apostasy had lasted more than a millennium when the sunlight of the gospel finally broke over the horizon, streaming across the earth. As Mönch joyously wrote:

> All now rejoice; the long night is o'er.
> Truth is on earth once more!
>
> Oh, how glorious from the throne above
> Shines the gospel light of truth and love!
> Bright as the sun, this heavenly ray
> Lights ev'ry land today.
> (*Hymns*, 1985, no. 264)

Sunshine for the Latter-day Saint Missionary Soul contains 101 stories and poems about people who have been warmed by and in turn have warmed others with the "heavenly ray" of the gospel of Jesus Christ. This newest volume in the beloved *Sunshine* series includes classic missionary stories of early Saints who raced forth on foot, horseback, and boat to the corners of the world to share the good news of the gospel with all people; recent stories of missionaries opening doors and hearts in new lands; and stories of the Lord's protecting and strengthening influence over his messengers of truth. It also includes a section that is perfect for

Latter-day Saints, young and old, who are preparing to serve full-time missions as well as sections for those involved in member missionary work and reactivation.

With contributions from such noted authors and missionaries as Anita R. Canfield, Parley P. Pratt, Marion D. Hanks, Dean Hughes, Robert E. Wells, George D. Durrant, Wilford Woodruff, Elaine Cannon, LeGrand Richards, and Ardeth Greene Kapp, *Sunshine for the Latter-day Saint Missionary Soul* is sure to encourage and inspire readers as they share the glorious light of the gospel with those who have walked in darkness.

The publisher expresses gratitude to the authors whose works make up this volume. The publisher also acknowledges and expresses thanks to Lesley Taylor for her help in selecting, compiling, and arranging the stories and poems for this book.

The Restoration and
the Book of Mormon

The Morning Breaks, The Shadows Flee

PARLEY P. PRATT

The morning breaks, the shadows flee;
Lo, Zion's standard is unfurled!
The dawning of a brighter day
Majestic rises on the world.

The clouds of error disappear
Before the rays of truth divine;
The glory bursting from afar
Wide o'er the nations soon will shine.

The Gentile fulness now comes in,
And Israel's blessings are at hand.
Lo, Judah's remnant, cleansed from sin,
Shall in their promised Canaan stand.

Jehovah speaks! Let earth give ear,
And Gentile nations turn and live.
His mighty arm is making bare
His cov'nant people to receive.

Angels from heav'n and truth from earth
Have met, and both have record borne;
Thus Zion's light is bursting forth
To bring her ransomed children home.

"*I* Felt Such a Desire to Read the Book"

MARY LIGHTNER

Quite a number of the residents of Kirtland accepted baptism. Mother and myself also, in the month of October, 1830. A branch of the Church was organized, and Father Morley was ordained an elder to preside over it. He owned a large farm, about a mile from Kirtland, and some three or four families went there to live, and meetings were held there. A good spirit and one of union prevailed among the brethren for some time.

After Oliver Cowdery and his brethren left there for Missouri on their mission to the Lamanites, a wrong spirit crept into our midst, and a few were led away by it. About this time, John Whitmer came and brought a Book of Mormon. There was a meeting that evening, and we learned that Brother Morley had the book in his possession—the only one in that part of the country.

I went to his house just before the meeting was to commence, and asked to see the book; Brother Morley put it in my hand; as I looked at it, I felt such a desire to read it, that I could not refrain from asking him to let me take it home and read it, while he attended meeting. He said it would be too late for me to take it back after meeting, and another thing, he had hardly had time to read a chapter in it himself, and but few of the brethren had even seen it, but I pled so earnestly for it, he finally said, "Child, if you will bring this book home before breakfast tomorrow morning, you may take it." He admonished me to be very careful, and see that no harm came to it.

If any person in this world was ever perfectly happy in the possession of any coveted treasure, I was when I had permission to read that wonderful book. Uncle and Aunt were Methodists, so when I got into the house, I exclaimed, "Oh, Uncle, I have got the 'Golden Bible.'" Well, there was consternation in the house for a few moments, and I was severely reprimanded for being so presumptuous as to ask such a favor, when Brother Morley had not read it himself. However, we all took turns reading it until very late in the night. As soon as it was light enough to see, I was up and learned the first verse in the book.

When I reached Brother Morley's they had been up for only a little while. When I handed him the book, he remarked, "I guess you did not read much in it." I showed him how far we had read. He was surprised and said, "I don't believe you can tell me one word of it." I then repeated the first verse, also the outlines of the history of Nephi. He gazed at me in surprise, and said, "Child, take this book home and finish it, I can wait."

Before or about the time I finished the last chapter, the Prophet Joseph Smith arrived in Kirtland, and moved into a part of Newel K. Whitney's house (Uncle Algernon's partner in the Mercantile Business), while waiting for his goods to be put in order. Brother Whitney brought the Prophet Joseph to our house and introduced him to the older ones of the family (I was not in at the time). In looking around he saw the Book of Mormon on the shelf, and asked how that book came to be there. He said, "I sent that book to Brother Morley."

Uncle told him how his niece had obtained it. He asked, "Where is your niece?" I was sent for; when he saw me he looked at me so earnestly, I felt almost afraid. After a moment or two he came and put his hands on my head and gave me a great blessing, the first I ever received, and made me a present of the book, and said he would give Brother Morley another. He came in time to rebuke the evil spirits, and set the Church in order. We all felt that he was a man of God, for he spoke with power, and as one having authority in very deed.

".A Very Strange Book"

PARLEY P. PRATT

In August, 1830, I had closed my business, completed my arrangements, and we bid adieu to our wilderness home and never saw it afterwards.

On settling up, at a great sacrifice of property, we had about ten dollars left in cash. With this small sum, we launched forth into the wide world, determining first to visit our native place, on our mission, and then such other places as I might be led to by the Holy Spirit. . . .

. . . Landing in Buffalo, we engaged our passage for Albany on a canal boat, distance 360 miles. This, including board, cost all our money and some articles of clothing.

Arriving at Rochester, I informed my wife that, notwithstanding our passage being paid through the whole distance, yet I must leave the boat and her to pursue her passage to our friends; while I would stop awhile in this region. Why, I did not know; but so it was plainly manifest by the Spirit to me. I said to her, "we part for a season; go and visit our friends in our native place; I will come soon, but how soon I know not; for I have a work to do in this region of country, and what it is, or how long it will take to perform it, I know not; but I will come when it is performed."

My wife would have objected to this; but she had seen the hand of God so plainly manifest in His dealings with me many times, that she dare not oppose the things manifest to me by His spirit.

She, therefore, consented; and I accompanied her as far as Newark, a small town upwards of 100 miles from Buffalo, and then took leave of her, and of the boat.

It was early in the morning, just at the dawn of day, I walked ten miles into the country, and stopped to breakfast with a Mr. Wells. I proposed to preach in the evening. Mr. Wells readily accompanied me through the neighborhood to visit the people, and circulate the appointment.

We visited an old Baptist deacon by the name of Hamlin. After hearing of our appointment for evening, he began to tell of a *book,* a STRANGE BOOK, a VERY STRANGE BOOK! in his possession, which had been just published. This book, he said, purported to have been originally written on plates either of gold or brass, by a branch of the tribes of Israel; and to have been discovered and translated by a young man near Palmyra, in the State of New York, by the aid of visions, or the ministry of angels. I inquired of him how or where the book was to be obtained. He promised me the perusal of it, at his house the next day, if I would call. I felt a strange interest in the book. I preached that evening to a small audience, who appeared to be interested in the truths which I endeavored to unfold to them in a clear and lucid manner from the Scriptures. Next morning I called at his house, where, for the first time, my eyes beheld the "BOOK OF MORMON"—that book of books—that record which reveals the antiquities of the *"New World"* back to the remotest ages, and which unfolds the destiny of its people and the world for all time to come;—that Book which contains the fulness of the gospel of a crucified and risen Redeemer;—that Book which reveals a lost remnant of Joseph, and which was the principal means, in the hands of God, of directing the entire course of my future life.

I opened it with eagerness, and read its title page. I then read the testimony of several witnesses in relation to the manner of its being found and translated. After this I commenced its contents by course. I read all day; eating was a burden, I had no desire for food; sleep was a burden when the night came, for I preferred reading to sleep.

As I read, the spirit of the Lord was upon me, and I knew and comprehended that the book was true, as plainly and manifestly as a man comprehends and knows that he exists. My joy was now full, as it were, and I rejoiced sufficiently to more than pay me for all the sorrows, sacrifices and toils of my life. I soon determined to see the young man who had been the instrument of its discovery and translation.

I accordingly visited the village of Palmyra, and inquired for the residence of Mr. Joseph Smith. I found it some two or three miles from the village. As I approached the house at the close of the day I overtook a man who was driving some cows, and inquired of him for Mr. Joseph Smith, the translator of the *"Book of Mormon."* He informed me that he now resided in Pennsylvania; some one hundred miles distant. I inquired for his father, or for any of the family. He told me that his father had gone a journey; but that his residence was a small house just before me; and, said he, I am his brother. It was Mr. Hyrum Smith. I informed him of the interest I felt in the Book, and of my desire to learn more about it. He welcomed me to his house, and we spent the night together; for neither of us felt disposed to sleep. We conversed most of the night, during which I unfolded to him much of my experience in my search after truth, and my success so far; together with that which I felt was lacking, viz: a commissioned priesthood, or apostleship to minister in the ordinances of God.

He also unfolded to me the particulars of the discovery of the Book; its translation; the rise of the Church of Latter-day Saints, and the commission of his brother Joseph, and others, by revelation and the ministering of angels, by which the apostleship and authority had been again restored to the earth. After duly weighing the whole matter in my mind I saw clearly that these things were true; and that myself and the whole world were without baptism, and without the ministry and ordinances of God; and that the whole world had been in this condition since the days that inspiration and revelation had ceased—in short, that this was a *new dispensation* or *commission,* in fulfilment of prophecy, and for the restoration of Israel, and to prepare the way before the second coming of the Lord.

In the morning I was compelled to take leave of this worthy man and his family—as I had to hasten back a distance of thirty miles, on foot, to fulfil an appointment in the evening. As we parted he kindly presented me with a copy of the Book of Mormon. I had not yet completed its perusal, and was glad indeed to possess a copy of my own. I travelled on a few miles, and, stopping to rest, I commenced again to read the book. To my great joy I found that Jesus Christ, in his glorified resurrected body, had appeared to the remnant of Joseph on the continent of America, soon after his resurrection and ascension into heaven; and that he also administered, in person, to the ten lost tribes; and that through his personal ministry in these countries his gospel was revealed and written in countries and among nations entirely unknown to the Jewish apostles.

Thus revealed, written, handed down and preserved, till revealed in this age by the angels of God, it had, of course, escaped the corruptions of the great and abominable church; and been preserved in purity.

This discovery greatly enlarged my heart, and filled my soul with joy and gladness. I esteemed the Book, or the information contained in it, more than all the riches of the world. Yes; I verily believe that I would not at that time have exchanged the knowledge I then possessed, for a legal title to all the beautiful farms, houses, villages and property which passed in review before me, on my journey through one of the most flourishing settlements of western New York.

$\mathcal{D}$mitry the Believer
Finds a Book

HOWARD L. BIDDULPH

$\mathbf{A}$ few days before Elders Richard Davis, Thomas Wright, Brandon Arrington, and Jesus Condori arrived to open a new city [in the Ukraine], an unusual event occurred. A professor at the state university named Dmitry discovered a strange book in a bookstore entitled *Kniga mormona* (the Book of Mormon in Russian).

A Russian born in Siberia, Dmitry was converted to Christianity while serving in the Soviet Red Army, where he read the New Testament. After completing military service, he attended the Russian Orthodox Seminary, where he was a brilliant student. Dmitry was unable to accept some of the doctrines and practices of the Russian Orthodox Church, so he was not ordained. As an unordained religious activist, he was arrested and spent three years in terrible prison camps.

After his release, Dmitry found opportunity during the more liberal Gorbachev era to teach a course at the university titled "The Bible As Literature," which was in actuality a course on biblical theology and religious philosophy. Since he was both a brilliant teacher and a believer, the principal churches in that area sent priests and ministers to be trained by him, in the absence of a theological seminary.

Then came the day in May when Dmitry discovered the Russian copy of the Book of Mormon in a local bookstore. Its impact upon him was somewhat like the experience of Parley P. Pratt. Dmitry read the book nonstop, and when he finished, he felt a deep conviction that he had indeed discovered "another testament of Jesus Christ."

A few days later he met Elder Wright and Elder Condori on the street, almost immediately after their arrival in the large city.

Dmitry suffered persecution for his conversion to the restored gospel. He was banned from teaching priests of the Russian Orthodox Church and also banned from entering any of its church buildings or facilities. The Orthodox bishop attempted to get the university rector to fire Dmitry because he had become a Latter-day Saint. Twice he was attacked by young thugs on the street, who beat him into unconsciousness and took his belongings.

Dmitry became the first branch president of the Church in his city and remains a devoted spiritual leader and teacher in the Church. Although living in great poverty, he is positive, loving, and full of faith in God.

"Do You Ever Cry When You Read the Book of Mormon?"

MARION G. ROMNEY

I remember reading [the Book of Mormon] with one of my lads when he was very young. On one occasion I lay in the lower bunk and he in the upper bunk. We were each reading aloud alternate paragraphs of those last three marvelous chapters of Second Nephi. I heard his voice breaking and thought he had a cold, but we went on to the end of the three chapters. As we finished he said to me, "Daddy, do you ever cry when you read the Book of Mormon?"

"Yes, Son," I answered. "Sometimes the Spirit of the Lord so witnesses to my soul that the Book of Mormon is true that I do cry."

"Well," he said, "that is what happened to me tonight."

The Voice of God Again Is Heard

EVAN STEPHENS

The voice of God again is heard,
The silence has been broken,
The curse of darkness is withdrawn,
The Lord from heav'n hath spoken.

Rejoice ye living and ye dead!
Rejoice, for your salvation
Begins anew this happy morn
Of final dispensation.

O messengers of truth, go forth,
Proclaim the gospel story,
Go forth the nations to prepare,
To greet the King of Glory.
Shout we hosanna, shout again,
Till all creation blending
Shall join in one great grand Amen
Of anthems never ending.

"What Is That Book?"

KEVIN STOKER

When Alberto C. Bulseco made the decision to be baptized, he knew it might mean the end of his marriage. But "I had feared God all my life," he says. "I could not reject that which I knew was true."

Alberto, who would later become president of the Sorsogon District of the Philippines Cebu East Mission, had been looking for the true church for most of his life. He first heard about the restored gospel during his summer vacation in 1980. "We stopped at the boardinghouse of my brother, who was then studying in Manila, to take a rest before proceeding further north [to where his parents lived]. I have two brothers, and we're very close. Whenever we meet, it has been our practice to discuss scriptures from the Bible and also to talk about religion. Since childhood we have been dissatisfied with the religion our parents taught."

His brother said Mormon missionaries were coming to their boardinghouse to visit one of the other residents. Alberto remembered reading about the Mormons in the past and knew they believed in an ancient, but progressive, civilization. As it happened, the person the missionaries were supposed to visit was not interested, so the two brothers entertained them instead.

The elders, one an American and the other a Filipino, started by teaching the young men to pray. Alberto offered the opening prayer. When he finished, the American missionary began explaining more about prayer, but Alberto's attention was drawn to a blue book half hidden under the Filipino elder's arm.

"I was curious," he recalls. "I interrupted the missionary and asked what the book was. They were somewhat hesitant to tell me, but I strongly felt that it had something to do with their belief." He asked for the book, promising to read it. The missionaries continued to stall, so Alberto insisted that he receive a copy and swore he would read it. The elders then gave him the book and explained a little about it before continuing their discussion.

That discussion largely went unheeded. "The next things they said were no longer important to me. I felt that this book would tell me all I needed to know from them. My enthusiasm to begin reading the Book of Mormon was so intense that I wanted to cut short my vacation."

When he and his wife and child returned home, he finally had time to read. As he opened the book, he felt some power in it that caused his fingers to tremble. "A marvelous feeling engulfed me as I read every line. I often had to repeat the words and verses just to savor the sweet and satisfying feeling that came from them. My inspiration in reading the Book of Mormon was very unusual. I almost never got tired and hungry. To eat was a burden. I woke up during the middle of the night just to read it."

No other book had caused him to weep as the Book of Mormon did. It seemed to quench his soul's thirst for spiritual truth. A month after starting it, he finished reading the book and wanted to be baptized. The missionaries in Manila had taken down his name and address and had promised to have other missionaries visit him. However, none had knocked on his door.

Finally, Alberto went searching for the missionaries. When he found them, he told them he wanted to be baptized. They were so surprised they thought Alberto was joking. But when Alberto testified of the truth of the Book of Mormon, the missionaries realized he was sincere. They began teaching him the discussions. His wife persecuted him for studying and threatened to leave him. But he said only God could stop him from being baptized.

On August 5, 1980, Alberto was baptized. "I felt a fulfillment I had never felt in my life," he said. Two years later his wife joined the Church, and they and their four children have been sealed in the temple. His parents, brothers, and one sister also have been converted. All these blessings he attributes to a faith kindled from reading the Book of Mormon.

The Cheapest Book in the Store

ROBERT E. WELLS

I listened to this experience at a stake conference as told by a member who had been asked to give his testimony about his conversion.

The brother said he rode to and from work about an hour each way on a company bus to a sugar mill outside of town. He liked to read books on the boring ride but did not have the money to buy new books. He had a favorite bookstore which also sold used and secondhand books. One day, with very little money, he entered the store and asked the owner what the cheapest big book was, of over two hundred pages, in the entire place.

The owner pointed to a box of very old books in a corner. "Those are about to be junked," he said. "The prices are marked, but I might even lower it more if you find something you like."

The interested reader dug through the box of dusty and discarded volumes. The cheapest one in the whole box was a very tattered, coverless, stained, but intact Book of Mormon. He bought it because it had over five hundred pages and was the cheapest book there. He had already read the Koran, the Talmud, and the Bible, so he thought the Book of Mormon would be as educational as any other religious book. He was a voracious reader and liked the printed word, he explained to the store owner.

On the bus he started to read the old, beaten Book of Mormon. He did not mind the double columns with every verse numbered, because he felt it gave a certain dignified importance to each thought. He did not mind the lack of illustrations, nor did he expect any in such a book. But the spirit of the contents intrigued him. He liked the old-fashioned and unique way the story began. He followed it carefully, pondering over what he was reading.

This fellow got all the way to 2 Nephi chapter 2, when something strange began stirring within him. . . .

The brother giving his conversion story went on to say that as he read in this chapter he felt an urge to pray to God for the first time in his adult life. He said he had gone to Mass as a boy with his mother until he was about twelve; then, since his father never went, he decided that he was grown up enough that he did not have to go to Mass nor pray anymore.

Now he offered a simple prayer to God in his mind, saying, *God, what is this book? What am I feeling? What am I supposed to do about it?*

He said his answer was nothing more than the impression to wait and God would tell him more. That night, the fellow was reading in his humble home when two missionaries on their way home felt a distinct inspiration to stop at his door. They followed the Spirit. As the man opened the door to their knock, the entry light fell on the Book of Mormon that one of the missionaries held in his hand in such a way that the title was easily visible to him. He exclaimed, "You've got my book!" The missionary held his book more tightly, thinking, "No, this is my book." The fellow explained, "No—it's just that I have never seen a Book of Mormon with a cover on it. Come on in! I want to talk to you." He later joined the Church.

"Burn the Book"

DON VINCENT DI FRANCESCA

As I think back over the events of my life leading up to a cold morning in February 1910, I cannot escape the feeling that God had been mindful of my existence. That morning the caretaker of the Italian chapel delivered a note to me from the pastor, advising me he was ill in bed and asking me to come to his house, as he had important matters to discuss with me regarding the affairs of the parish.

As I walked down Broadway [in New York City], the strong wind from the open sea blew cold against me, so I held my head down and turned my face away from the wind. It was then I saw what appeared to be a book lying on top of an open barrel of ashes, set there to be picked up by the garbage collection wagon. The form of the pages and the manner in which they were bound gave me the impression that it was a religious book. Curious, I picked up the book and knocked it against the side of the barrel to shake the ashes from its pages. The book was written in the English language. I looked for the frontispiece, but it had been torn away.

As I stood there with the book in my hands, the fury of the wind turned the pages, and one by one, the names Nephi, Mosiah, Alma, Moroni, and Isaiah appeared before my eyes. Since the cold wind was bitter, I hurriedly wrapped the soiled book in a newspaper and continued my journey.

At the parish house I gave a few words of comfort to my colleague Scarillo and agreed to the services he requested of me during his illness. As I walked back to my own lodgings, my mind dwelt on the book in my hand and the strange names I had read. Who were these men? Who was this prophet Isaiah? Was he the one I had read about in the Bible, or was he some other Isaiah?

Back in my room I carefully turned the torn pages and came to the words of Isaiah, which I read most carefully. What could be the name of the church that taught such doctrine in words so easily understood? The cover of the book and the title page were missing. I read the declaration of witnesses in the opening pages and was strongly impressed by the strength of their testimonies, but there was no other clue to the book's identity.

I purchased some alcohol and cotton from the drugstore beneath my lodgings and began cleaning the soiled pages. Then for several hours I read what was written in the book. When I had read chapter ten of the book of Moroni, I locked the door of my room; and with the book held in my hands, I knelt down and asked God, the Eternal Father, in the name of his Son Jesus Christ, to tell me if the book was of God. As I prayed, I felt my body becoming cold. Then my heart began to pound, and a feeling of warmth and gladness came over me and filled me with such joy that I cannot find words to express. I knew that the words of the book came from God.

I continued my services in the parish, but my preaching was tinged with the new words I had found in the book. The members of my congregation were so interested in my words that they became dissatisfied with the sermons of my colleagues, and they asked them why they did not preach the sweet arguments of Don Vincent. This was the beginning of troubles for me. When members began leaving the chapel during the sermons of my colleagues and remained when I occupied the pulpit, my colleagues became angry with me.

The beginning of real discord began Christmas eve, 1910. In my sermon that evening, I told the story of the birth and mission of Jesus Christ as given in my new book. When I had finished, some of my colleagues, without any shadow of shame, publicly contradicted all I had said. The absurdities of their assertions so upset me that I openly rebelled against them. They denounced me and turned me over to the committee of censure for disciplinary action.

When I appeared before this committee, the members gave me what was supposed to be fatherly advice. They counseled me to burn the book, which they said was of the devil, since it was the cause of so much trouble and had destroyed the harmony of the pastoral brothers. I replied by giving my witness that the book they asked me to burn was the word of God, but because of the missing pages I did not know the name of the church that had brought forth the book. I declared that if I were to burn the book, I would displease God. I would rather go out of the congregation of the church than offend him. When I had so stated, the president of the council ended the discussion, stating the council would decide on the matter later.

It was not until 1914 that I was once again brought before the council. The vice venerable spoke in a friendly tone, suggesting that the sharp words of the committee members at the previous hearing may have provoked me, which was regrettable, since they all loved me and were mindful of the valuable assistance I had always so freely given. However, he said, I must remember that obedience—complete and absolute—is the rule. The long suffering of the members, to whom I had continued to preach falsehoods, had come to an end, and I must burn the book.

In reply, I stated I could not deny the words of the book nor would I burn it, since in doing so I would offend God. I said I looked forward with joy to the time when the church to which the book belonged would be made known to me and I would become a part of it. At this, the vice venerable cried, "Enough! Enough!" He then read the decision that had been made by the council: I was to be stripped of my position as a pastor of the church and of every right and privilege I had previously enjoyed.

Three weeks later I was called before the supreme synod. After giving me an opportunity to retract my previous statements, which I refused to do, the synod confirmed the judgment of the council. I was thus completely cut off from the body of the church.

In November 1914 I was called into the Italian army and sent to the Port of Naples. I saw action in France, where I experienced all of the sadness and suffering associated with the battles of World War I. Remembering the lessons of the book I had read, I related to some of the men in my company the story of the people of Ammon—how they refused to shed the blood of their brothers and buried their arms rather than be guilty of so great crimes. The chaplain reported me to the colonel, and the next day I was escorted to the colonel's office. He asked me to tell him the story I had related to the soldiers, as it is recorded in the twenty-fourth chapter of Alma. Then he asked me how I had come into possession of the book, and why I retained a book written in the English language and published by an unnamed church. I received as punishment a ten-day sentence on bread and water, with the order that I was to speak no more of the book and its stories.

After the end of the war I returned to New York, where I met an old friend who was a pastor of my former church and who knew the history of my troubles. He felt I had been unfairly dealt with, and he began interceding for me with members of the synod. I was finally admitted to the congregation as a lay member. As an experiment, it was agreed that I should accompany one of the pastors on a mission to New Zealand and to Australia.

In Sydney, Australia, we met some Italian immigrants who asked questions about the errors in the translations of the Bible as published by the Catholic Church. They were not satisfied with the answers given by my companion, and he became angry with them. Then they asked me about it, and, knowing I had the truth in the Book of Mormon, I once again told the story of Christ's appearance to the people of the land described there, and that Christ had said, "That other sheep I have which are not of this fold; them also I must bring, and they shall hear my voice; and there shall be one fold, and one shepherd." (3 Ne. 15:17.) When they asked me where I had learned such teachings, I told them of the book I had found. The story was sweet to them but very bitter for my colleague. He reported me to the synod, and once again their previous judgment was confirmed, and I was cut off from the church forever. Soon after, I returned to Italy.

In May 1930, while I was seeking in a French dictionary for some information, I suddenly saw the entry "Mormon." I read the words carefully and found that a Mormon Church had been established in 1830 and that this church operated a university at Provo, Utah. I wrote to the president of the university at Provo, asking for information about the book and its missing pages. I received an answer two weeks later, and was told that my letter had been passed on to the President of The Church of Jesus Christ of Latter-day Saints and that he would inform me about the book with the missing pages, which book did indeed belong to the Mormon Church.

On June 16, 1930, President Heber J. Grant answered my letter and sent a copy of the Book of Mormon, which had been translated into the Italian language in 1852 by President Lorenzo Snow while he was a missionary. President Grant informed me that Elder John A. Widtsoe was president of the Church's European Mission, with headquarters in Liverpool, England, and he would give my request to him. A few days later, Elder Widtsoe wrote to me from Liverpool and sent me a pamphlet that contained the story of the Prophet Joseph Smith, telling of the gold plates and the coming forth of the Book of Mormon. At long last I had learned the rest of the story begun so long ago when, guided by the hand of God, I found the torn book lying on top of a barrel of ashes on a street in New York City.

On June 5, 1932, Elder Widtsoe came to Naples to baptize me, but a revolution between the Fascists and anti-Fascists on the island of Sicily had broken out, and the police at Palermo refused permission for me to leave the island. I was thus denied a chance for baptism at that time.

The following year Elder Widtsoe asked me to translate the Joseph Smith pamphlet into Italian and to have 1,000 copies published. I took my translation to a printer, Joseph Gussio, who took the material to the Catholic bishop of the diocese of Cefalu. The bishop ordered the printer to destroy the material. I brought suit against the printer, but all I received from the court was an order to him to return the original booklet, which he had thrown into some waste paper in a cellar.

When Elder Widtsoe was released as president of the mission in 1934, I started correspondence with Elder Joseph F. Merrill, who had succeeded him. He put my name on the mailing list for the *Millennial Star,* which I received until 1940 when the subscription was stopped because of World War II. In January 1937, Elder Richard R. Lyman, successor to President Merrill, wrote to me, advising me that he and Elder Hugh B. Brown would be in Rome on a certain day and I could meet them there and be baptized. The letter was delayed because of war conditions, and I did not receive it in time.

From then until 1949, I was cut off from all news of the Church, but I remained a faithful follower and preached the gospel of the dispensation of the fulness of times. I had copies of the standard works, and I translated chapters into Italian and sent them to acquaintances with the greeting: "Good day. The morning breaks—Jehovah speaks!"

On February 13, 1949, I resumed correspondence with Elder Widtsoe at Church headquarters in Salt Lake City. Elder Widtsoe answered my letter October 3, 1950, explaining that he had been in Norway. I sent him a long letter in reply in which I asked him to help me to be quickly baptized, because I felt that I had proven myself to be a faithful son and pure servant of God, observing the laws and commandments of his kingdom. Elder Widtsoe asked President Samuel E. Bringhurst of the Swiss Mission if he would go to Sicily to baptize me. On January 18, 1951, President Bringhurst arrived on the island, and I was baptized at Imerese, Province of Palermo. According to the records of the Church, this was apparently the first baptism performed on the Island of Sicily. Then on April 28, 1956, I entered the temple at Bern, Switzerland, and received my endowments.

At last, to be in the presence of my Heavenly Father! I felt I had now proved faithful in my second estate, after having searched for and found the true Church by means of an unknown book that I found so many years ago, lying on an open barrel of ashes in the city of New York.

Faith and Prayer

A Prayer for Five Shillings

AMASA POTTER

We had labored a few weeks in this city [in Australia] and had baptized a few into the Church, when we received a letter from Emue Plains, stating that the people would like to see and hear a "Mormon" Elder. Emue Plains was a distance of sixty miles from where we were, and when we started it had been raining about a week, and a great portion of the country was flooded with water. We had a large river to cross on the way, and we were informed that the bridge had been carried off and there was a ferry established across the river which charged five shillings each passenger. We did not have any money with which to pay this charge, and my companion was anxious to know what we should do for money to pay the ferriage with. We were then about three miles from the ferry, and were passing through timber. I told him that we would go into the woods and pray to God to open the heart of some one to give it to us. We did so, and we had traveled but a short distance through a lane between two fields, when we looked ahead of us a little way and saw an old man coming across the field. He came into the road ahead of us, and as he came to meet us he had a smile on his countenance. He reached out his hand to me, as if to shake hands, and left a crown, or five shilling piece, in my hand and went to my companion and did the same; but spoke not a word. I cannot describe the feeling that we had when the man took hold of our hands; we felt our hearts burn within us, and it did not seem that we had power to ask him his name or where he was from, as we usually did when a person gave us any article of clothing or money. He was a man about six feet high, well proportioned, and wore a suit of light gray clothes and a broad-brimmed hat, and his hair and beard were about eighteen inches long and as white as snow. We passed on and came to the ferry, and the money that we had was just enough to pay our ferriage.

We came to Emue Plains, labored and preached one month, baptized twenty-one persons and organized a branch of the Church. So you see that our Heavenly Father opened up our way to preach the gospel.

Valentina's Faith

HOWARD L. BIDDULPH

Valentina is a senior citizen [in the Ukraine] who had drunk strong coffee for several years as a prescription from her doctor for a health condition. When she was preparing for baptism into The Church of Jesus Christ of Latter-day Saints, Valentina read of the Word of Wisdom and what it said about coffee. She returned to her doctor and asked if there might be a prescription that would permit her to take something other than coffee for her condition. The doctor said that he knew of nothing available and that if that were true she should continue drinking the coffee. She scoured the woefully depleted pharmacies throughout the city and found that there were no other stimulants available that would meet her needs.

Valentina might have concluded that in the absence of other remedies she was justified in taking coffee purely for medicinal purposes, as her doctor prescribed. It troubled her, however, to fail to fulfill anything given of the Lord. "I don't want to miss any of the spiritual blessings the Lord has promised in this revelation. I want to be an example to my family, who are all unbelievers. How can I do that if they see me drink coffee each day?"

After prayerful consideration, Valentina approached the missionaries who had taught her the gospel. "If you will give me a blessing through the priesthood, I believe Heavenly Father will take away my health problems. Whatever his will might be, however, I have decided that I will never drink tea or coffee again. I trust in the words of our Savior."

Valentina received a wonderful blessing, promising her health and spiritual gifts through her faith. She was then baptized, and immediately her health problem disappeared. She has often publicly borne her testimony about this experience and of the spiritual and temporal blessings that the Lord granted her through obedience to his commandments.

$\mathcal{L}$ed by the Spirit

JOHN D. WHETTEN

While on my mission I went to a zone conference where the mission president told a story about Elder Parley P. Pratt dedicating Toronto, Canada, to the Lord. Then I went back to my missionary labors, having been a senior companion for only a few months. My companion and I chose a wooded area in the middle of Corby, England, about the size of eight Salt Lake City blocks. After fasting . . . we rode our bikes through the woods, praying for any small impression or faint feeling as to which way we should go. On the other side of the woods was a new area that we had never tracted before. There we stopped. "How do you feel about this area, Elder?" "I feel good about it." "So do I." "So, let's ride through it."

We rode down the major street, which had most of the streets leading off from it. On every block, we would stop and hold a conference. "How do you feel about this street?" "Oh, I don't feel anything." Then we would go on to the next one. "How do you feel about this street?" "Oh, not much."

This is how we went through the whole area. Finally, we got to about the next to the last street. Our faith was beginning to waver. "How do you feel about this street?" "I feel good about this street." "So do I." We went all the way down that street, which was about half a mile long. We were trying to be led to somebody.

If we started tracting at the wrong end of the street, we could miss the individual we felt the Lord had prepared. At the end of the street, we both felt we should start at the other end, so we went back up. Then we had another decision. Which side of the street should we start on? We both felt we should start on the opposite side of the street, so we went over.

An old lady came to the first door we knocked on. We said, "Good morning, we have been sent here by Jesus Christ with an important message for you. May we come in and share that message with you?" She replied, "Yes, I would like that." We went in and taught her the gospel.

We later learned how earnestly she had been praying the last two days that she might gain a knowledge of Jesus Christ and his church. . . . She was baptized. And the Lord led us to many more families that month in answer to our prayers.

First Prayer

DEAN HUGHES AND TOM HUGHES

In 1963, Mary Ellen Edmunds and Carol Smithen became the first missionaries to work in Quezon City in the Philippines. Later the city would become the headquarters of an entire mission, but at the time it was part of the Philippines Zone of the Southern Far East Mission. Eventually Sister Smithen received a new companion, and Mary Jane Davidson was assigned to work with Sister Edmunds.

Early the next year, Sister Edmunds and Sister Davidson were going door to door "tracting," and they were not doing very well. They really weren't in the mood to work that morning, and they knew what that meant: they didn't have the Spirit. So they stopped on the street, each said a silent prayer, and then they approached the next house. When they rang the doorbell, an eye soon appeared in a little peephole. The sisters told the man on the other side of the peephole that they were missionaries and would like to visit with him for a few minutes.

"I am Cat-o-leek," the man said. At that time, the missionaries did not learn the Filipino languages as they do now. Most people did speak at least some English, but the sisters could tell that this man did not speak a great deal. They both felt strongly prompted, however, to keep trying, and finally he agreed to let them come in.

The man told the sisters that his name was Felixberto S. Ocampo. He was a somewhat older man with an impressive appearance and dark, graying hair. That hair, along with his kindly manner, reminded the sisters of President David O. McKay.

As the sisters sat down to talk with Mr. Ocampo, the Spirit was telling both of them not to present a lesson but to tell him about Joseph Smith's first vision. And so Sister Edmunds told the story, using simple English words so that he could understand. As she spoke, however, she was struck by the way he listened with full attention and great interest.

When Sister Edmunds finished the story, Mr. Ocampo's response was unlike any she had experienced before. "That is a beautiful story," he said. "Can you tell me again?"

This time Sister Davidson gave the account, and again the missionaries were moved by the great concentration and the conviction in Mr. Ocampo's eyes. This time his reply was even more surprising: "This is a very beautiful story. Can you tell me one more time?"

The missionaries had to take turns this time. They were so moved by the spirit of this good man, the obvious joy he was receiving in hearing about Joseph Smith, that neither could talk very long without crying. When they made it through the story the third time, Mr. Ocampo asked, "Where is he now?"

The sisters told him that Joseph Smith was dead, and they were amazed to see how saddened Mr. Ocampo appeared. He had just heard the wonderful news that God had spoken to a man on earth, and now he was disappointed and sorrowful to learn that this prophet was already gone. He then asked, "How did he die?" The sisters were deeply hurt to have to tell him that Joseph Smith had been murdered.

"*Why?* Why did they do this?" Mr. Ocampo asked, with pain in his voice and in his eyes. . . .

"If I have been alive," Mr. Ocampo said, in his halting English, "I will protect his life with my life."

Sister Edmunds and Sister Davidson reassured Mr. Ocampo that a prophet was, in fact, still upon the earth, and they promised to return and continue to teach him. When they arrived for their second visit, Mr. Ocampo told them, "Oh, Sisters, I have a beautiful story to tell you." What he told them was the account he had read in a pamphlet that they had given him during their first visit. It was the story of Joseph Smith's vision along with other events in his life. He rehearsed the story in such detail that they could tell he had read it many times. . . .

During one visit, the sisters asked Mr. Ocampo whether he prayed. "Oh, yes, sisters," he said (pronouncing the word "seesters"). "I pray every day." So they taught him the principles of prayer and, from that time on, asked him to pray at the beginning or end of their meetings. He asked each time if it would be all right if he prayed in Tagalog, his own language. They said that was fine. They didn't understand much of what he said in these prayers, but they felt his good spirit.

Mr. Ocampo received all the missionary lessons with the same spirit, and he accepted baptism. One Sunday soon after he was baptized, the branch president asked him to pray in Church, but Brother Ocampo said he couldn't. The sisters were surprised. When they visited him the next time, he explained. "I want to pray the way *you* pray," he said, and it was only then that they discovered he had been saying memorized prayers, not speaking to the Lord in his own words.

The sisters repeated for him the elements of a prayer, and this time he understood. The idea that he could actually talk with his Heavenly Father was wonderful to him. "I'll be the one to pray this time," he told the sisters. "I'll use English. If I say something wrong, you can tell me."

They knelt together, and then he paused for a very long time as he considered what he wanted to say. This was no ordinary event, the sisters realized; this man of faith was about to converse with the Lord for the first time. He wanted to choose the right words. Both sisters were weeping before Brother Ocampo even began to pray.

He worked hard for the right English words as he began, but the sisters felt no need to correct anything he said. Now and again he would stop and say, "Sisters, this is very beautiful, no?"

They would nod, tears streaming down their faces. This was clearly the most beautiful prayer either had ever heard.

"If I am slow, will He wait for me?" he asked at one point.

"Yes," the sisters told him. "Take all the time you want."

And finally he asked, "Sisters, does Heavenly Father know Tagalog?"

They assured him that the Lord knew every language, and in response Brother Ocampo asked whether he could finish in his own language. They said he could, and then they heard him pour out his feelings fluently, in his native tongue, and they understood the spirit of what he said.

Brother Ocampo was a steadfast member of the Church until he died. His faith was a power to all who knew him.

"*He* Is Breathing His Last!"

ELIZA R. SNOW

At the close of his mission, [Lorenzo Snow] was appointed to take charge of a company of Saints, consisting of about two hundred and fifty souls, *en route* for Nauvoo; and in January, 1843, embarked on the ship "Swanton." The commander, Captain Davenport, and officers of the crew were kind and courteous, which contributed much to ameliorate the discomfort incident to life on the ocean.

The steward, a German by birth, was a young man, very affable in manner, and gentlemanly in deportment—a general favorite and highly respected by all. During the latter part of the voyage he took sick, and continued growing worse and worse, until death seemed inevitable. All means proved unavailing, and the captain, by whom he was much beloved, gave up all hope of his recovery, and requested the officers and crew to go in, one by one, and take a farewell look of their dying friend, which they did silently and solemnly, as he lay unconscious and almost breathless on his dying couch.

Immediately after this sad ceremony closed, one of our sisters, by the name of Martin, without my brother's knowledge, went to the captain and requested him to allow my brother to lay hands on the steward, according to our faith and practice under such circumstances, saying that she believed that the steward would be restored. The captain shook his head, and told her that the steward was now breathing his last, and it would be useless to trouble Mr. Snow. But Sister Martin was not to be defeated; she not only importuned, but earnestly declared her faith in the result of the proposed administration, and he finally yielded and gave consent.

As soon as the foregoing circumstance was communicated to my brother, he started toward the cabin where the steward lay, and in passing through the door met the captain, who was in tears. He said, "Mr. Snow, it is too late; he is expiring, he is breathing his last!" My brother made no reply, but took a seat beside the dying man. After devoting a few moments to secret prayer, he laid his hands on the head of the young man, prayed, and in the name of Jesus Christ rebuked the disease and commanded him to be made whole. Very soon after, to the joy and astonishment of all, he was seen walking the deck, praising and glorifying God for his restoration. The officers and sailors acknowledged the miraculous power of God, and on landing at New Orleans several of them were baptized, also the first mate, February 26, 1843.

"Welcome and Welcome!"

RENDELL N. MABEY AND GORDON T. ALLRED

Hang on!" someone warned. For an instant we were airborne as the taxi careened over a tooth-jarring strip of washboard and descended into the swale ahead. It was a hot day as usual, sweltering inside the cab even with the windows open, and the road was murderous. . . .

"If only we had a little rain to cool things off," Rachel said. "Anything to get some relief from this heat."

"Rainy season's coming up," Ted reminded her. "Once that happens we'll be getting more water than we bargained for."

Sitting there in front next to the window, I laughed a bit wearily, leaned forward to free the shirt from my sweating back, and grabbed for the dash as we jolted over another chuckhole. . . . Rachel, my wife of forty-five years, was in the back with our companions, Edwin Q. (Ted) Cannon, Jr., and his wife, Janath. To my left was E. D. Ukwat, better known as Daniel—our newfound guide, interpreter, devoted friend, and investigator. His skin, like the driver's, was very dark, and his forehead was beaded with perspiration. As usual, however, despite the growing discomfort, he was smiling and full of cheer. . . .

That morning . . . we had embarked from Calabar in a fast open boat with an outboard motor, traversing the mighty Cross River near its mouth in a one-hour journey to Oron. There we had hired the taxi and continued our quest, often with only the vaguest sense of direction. Addresses in that locale were nonexistent—merely the primitive-sounding names of tiny villages like Idung Imoh, Oding, Anang, and Okom . . . merely the knowledge that they were somewhere out there, people who were patiently waiting, who had been waiting throughout the years and praying for a miracle.

It was difficult at the moment to comprehend that we were a part of that miracle even though our efforts of the day had already met with gratifying success. For now, it was simply a matter of keeping body, soul, and vehicle together. Rounding a bend at one point, we narrowly escaped head-on collision with a truck. The road was hardly designed for two-way traffic, and driver's education was clearly not top priority in Nigeria, facts well attested to by the number of demolished vehicles along the wayside.

By now, however, we were encountering a few more natives, either cycling or afoot, and another small settlement had materialized. "Village Isighe," Daniel said. He smiled, displaying a set of prominent white teeth. "This is it—the one we've been looking for!"

All of us craned our necks, peering and exclaiming with surprise and relief. Just off the road was a rectangular white sign with neat block letters spelling: "Church of Jesus Christ of Latter-day Saints, Inc." The name of the village was just beneath. "And there, if I'm not mistaken," Ted said moments later, "is the chapel."

"That's it, all right," I agreed, "practically in our laps." Only fifty or sixty feet away was a primitive little meetinghouse plastered with dried mud: hardly likely to win any prizes in architecture or to insure cool and comfort in such weather, but a literal delight to behold even so.

It was now one o'clock Saturday afternoon, but a good many people were leaving the premises, filing from the doorway and wandering down the little lanes much as though they had just completed a sacrament meeting. Men, women, and children all dressed in their Sunday best, some in white, others in exotic colors, were passing by as we left the taxi. A number had stopped, in fact, to stare. Their dark, lustrous eyes were full of wonderment, and some of them seemed too astonished to return our words of greeting.

"I wonder what's going on," Janath said. "Church meetings on

Saturday?" Daniel smiled and shrugged, shaking his head, but it soon appeared that he was not a total stranger there.

"Some kind of meeting, obviously," I said. Even more obviously, we had just discovered another of those self-styled branches of the Church, growing independently for now like slips from the wild olive. More people who had learned about the gospel from an article in the *Reader's Digest,* letters to Salt Lake City, tracts, occasional copies of the Book of Mormon, or a passing visitor. Such congregations understood certain important principles of the restored gospel in most cases, enough to hunger and thirst for more, but their knowledge was meager and primitive. . . .

Moments after leaving our taxi, we were greeted by several men in colorful native robes, clearly religious leaders of some kind. Foremost among them was a wiry little man who introduced himself as Evangelist B. J. Ekong, head of the so-called LDS churches in Isighe and several other villages of that general area. His eyes were alert, full of intense expectation, and he smiled radiantly as though the purpose of our visit had already been revealed. "How truly wonderful!" he exclaimed, and he began seizing our hands. "Praise be to the Lord! Welcome! Welcome!" . . .

. . . "Well, we're very happy to be here," Ted said. "Looks as though you've just been holding a meeting of some kind."

"Yes, yes indeed," came the reply. Those with him nodded, beaming as though they shared some marvelous secret. "We must go ring the bell and summon our people to return immediately!"

"Oh, I don't think that's necessary for the moment," I began, but the Evangelist was irrepressible; all of them were filled with the same explosive spirit.

"Ah, but you don't quite understand," he persisted. "We really must ring the bell! The members of this congregation have been waiting for years. They have just completed a twenty-four-hour fast, praying to the Lord that his missionaries would come."

It is impossible to articulate the feelings of that moment, but the bell itself seemed full of rejoicing, and within minutes of our arrival we were seated in positions of honor before a congregation of approximately seventy-five people. All of them, even the smallest infants, seemed to observe our every movement and expression with fascination, and the Evangelist B. J. Ekong arose to offer his welcome in English.

"We have awaited this glad day for many years," he said, speaking in tones of great humility and dignity. "Now, very suddenly and without notice . . ." He hesitated, eyes glistening. "Now, very suddenly, you are here among us. You are here to bring that light and knowledge we so greatly desire and to show us the paths we must follow." He then turned to us more fully, making a slight bow and sweeping gesture with one hand. "For such a blessing we must thank our Father in Heaven everlastingly. Welcome, beloved and honored friends—welcome and welcome!"

I then arose as our senior representative and, with Daniel Ukwat to interpret, thanked all those present for their great devotion to the Lord, their interest and hospitality. . . . "We bring you greetings from our prophet Spencer W. Kimball in Salt Lake City. We bring you word of his great love and prayers and are here today in that same spirit, convinced that we are all children of God and therefore literal brothers and sisters." I testified as well to the divinity of our Savior, explained briefly the mission of Joseph Smith, and bore witness of the fact that we were duly authorized representatives of the only true church upon this earth, an organization constantly sustained by the lifeblood of prophetic revelation.

. . . Despite the necessity of an interpreter, we were "coming through." The Spirit of God, which in times of faith may transcend all other barriers, was bearing record. I could see it in their eyes and feel it in my veins, a conviction that steadily expanded as Elder Cannon and our wives in turn arose to unite their testimonies with my own. Last of all, Daniel himself attested to the fact that we were true messengers, divinely appointed to this mission.

At the conclusion of our remarks, various leaders from among the gathering arose to add their welcome and to ask questions. . . . Above all else, they desired assurance that we had not come as mere birds of passage, that never again would they be left in the wilderness, comfortless and alone. "In time past," an old man said, "a member or two of your religion have appeared among us, but only for a fleeting moment. They brought us greetings in one breath and said farewell with the next. We were tempted with the truth only to have it snatched away again. No one returned, and our letters to Salt Lake City received little reply." His eyes smoldered, but the fire was quenched with tears. "Will it also be the same with you?"

I shook my head, finding it difficult to respond. "We can appreciate your feelings," I said, "and greatly regret that you have been kept waiting so long. It must have been a terrible frustration, but God has many ways of testing the faithful, and perhaps this has been one of them. . . . But your prayers have been answered."

"Yes," Ted agreed. "This is the beginning. The restored gospel has come to Black Africa."

$\mathscr{A}$ Prayer for a Font of Water

GRANT H. TAYLOR

Brother Schmidt had met with many of the best elders ever to serve in the Danish Mission and had received the discussions several times over a three-year period. His wife was a member but not a strong influence either for or against the Church. He had read all of the standard works and more Church-related books than most of the missionaries even knew existed. He loved his wife and infant son and wanted something eternal for his family. But at the last minute, something always seemed to keep him from the baptismal commitment.

We had met with Brother Schmidt several times when he admitted to us and to himself that he had known for over a year that the restored gospel was true. We were elated when he told us that he knew it was time to act on that knowledge and set a baptismal date. We made arrangements for the following Saturday afternoon.

Saturday morning we rode our bikes to the Aalborg chapel and met our district leader and his companion. The baptism wouldn't take place until 3:00 P.M., but since it took several hours to fill the font, they would turn the water on at 10:00 A.M. to have it ready in time. Not needed there, my companion and I decided to take an early train to the Schmidt home in Hjorring (thirty miles north of Aalborg) to help Sister Schmidt with any final preparations as she waited for her husband to return from work.

When we arrived Sister Schmidt was very cool towards us. She said that Brother Schmidt wasn't ready for baptism and that we had pressured him into making a commitment. She further announced that he would be working late and could not meet the baptismal appointment.

Heartsick, we left the home but decided to wait across the street for Brother Schmidt to return so that we could talk with him about his decision. As we waited, we prayed with all our might for a solution to this problem.

When Brother Schmidt returned, nearly two hours after the time of his scheduled baptism, we crossed the street and knocked on the door. He let us in, but the Spirit had left him. He began apologizing but made it clear that his wife had convinced him that he was not yet ready to be baptized.

With a prayer in our hearts, we reviewed the simple truths of the gospel that we had taught him. We spoke of the importance of temple blessings for his family, which could come only after baptism. After bearing our testimonies, we persuaded him to kneel and pray with us. I prayed first and then asked him to pray. He was reluctant, but he bowed his head and said nothing for several minutes. When he finally spoke, he asked the Lord to let him know if he was ready for baptism. As he prayed, we felt the warm tingle of the Spirit, and we knew he and his wife had felt it.

When he finished, we all stood and nobody spoke for several moments. I told Brother Schmidt that there was no need to wait any longer.

He looked at me and smiled. "Let's go," he said.

In minutes we were on the way to Aalborg, all packed tightly into the Schmidts' little car. It was then the terrible realization hit me—he could not possibly be baptized that night.

To protect against the chance of children's falling into the water, there was a strict policy in the Aalborg District that the water not be left in the font overnight after a Saturday baptism. It was now 9:00 P.M., six hours after the scheduled time for the baptism. In all our worries, we had not thought to contact the district leader to let him know of the change in plans. And because there was no phone in the chapel, there was no way to stop and call him. Surely, the font was now empty, and Brother Schmidt would not be baptized that night.

I looked at my companion and saw that he was not aware of the problem. I thought of telling him and the Schmidts, but I didn't want to damage the enthusiasm that Brother Schmidt was finally feeling for baptism. I silently prayed that a miracle would happen—that somehow this baptism might take place.

As we rounded the last corner before the driveway to the Aalborg chapel, I saw that the outside light was still on. To my surprise, sitting on the cement steps in front of the chapel was the district leader and his companion. We got out of the car and I raced to the district leader, not daring to ask about the water.

He simply said, "I knew you were coming. The font is still full."

Brother Schmidt's baptism was late, but it was a marvelous experience for all of us. Through this experience I came to know the power of prayer, a power I cannot deny.

"How Shall I Know?"

JACOB HAMBLIN

In February, 1842, a neighbor called at my house and told me that he had heard a "Mormon" Elder preach. He asserted that he preached more Bible doctrine than any other man he had ever listened to, and that he knew what he preached was true. He claimed that the gospel had been restored to the earth, and that it was the privilege of all who heard it to know and understand it for themselves.

What this neighbor told me so influenced my mind, that I could scarcely attend to my ordinary business.

The Elder had left an appointment to preach again at the same place, and I went to hear him. When I entered the house he had already commenced his discourse. I shall never forget the feeling that came over me when I saw his face and heard his voice. He preached that which I had long been seeking for; I felt that it was indeed the gospel.

The principles he taught appeared so plain and natural, that I thought it would be easy to convince any one of their truth. In closing his remarks, the Elder bore testimony to the truth of the gospel.

The query came to my mind: How shall I know whether or not these things are so, and be satisfied? As if the Spirit prompted him to answer my inquiry, he again arose to his feet and said: "If there is anyone in the congregation who wishes to know how he can satisfy himself of the truth of these things, I can assure him that if he will be baptized, and have hands laid upon him for the gift of the Holy Ghost, he shall have an assurance of their truth."

This so fired up my mind, that I at once determined to be

baptized, and that too, if necessary, at the sacrifice of the friendship of my kindred and of every earthly tie.

I immediately went home and informed my wife of my intentions.

She told me that if I was baptized into the "Mormon" Church, I need not expect her to live with me any more.

The evening after the Elder had preached I went in search of him, and found him quite late at night. I told him my purpose, and requested him to give me a "Mormon Bible." He handed me the Old and New Testament.

I said, "I thought you had a new Bible." He then explained about the coming forth of the Book of Mormon, and handed me a copy of it.

The impressions I received at the time cannot be forgotten. The spirit rested upon me and bore testimony of its truth, and I felt like opening my mouth and declaring it to be a revelation from God.

On the 3rd of March, 1842, as soon as it was light in the morning, I started for a pool of water where I had arranged to meet with the Elder, to attend to the ordinance of baptism. On the way, the thought of the sacrifice I was making of wife, of father, mother, brothers, sister and numerous other connections, caused my resolution to waver.

As my pace slackened, some person appeared to come from above, who, I thought, was my grandfather. He seemed to say to me, "Go on, my son; your heart cannot conceive, neither has it entered into your mind to imagine the blessings that are in store for you, if you go on and continue in this work."

I lagged no more, but hurried to the pool, where I was baptized by Elder Lyman Stoddard.

It was said in my confirmation, that the spirits in prison greatly rejoiced over what I had done. I told Elder Stoddard my experience on my way to the water.

He then explained to me the work there was for me to do for my fathers, if I was faithful, all of which I believed and greatly rejoiced in.

On my way home, I called at the house of one of my neighbors. The family asked me if I had not been baptized by the "Mormon" Elder. I replied that I had. They stated that they believed what he preached to be the truth, and hoped they might have the opportunity of being baptized.

The following day Elder Stoddard came to my house, and told me that he had intended to leave the country, but could not go without coming to see me. For what purpose he had come, he knew not.

I related to him what my neighbors had said. He held more meetings in the place, and organized a branch before leaving.

$\mathscr{R}$eal Intent

ELDER "C"

Not all of a missionary's "contacts" come from knocking on doors. This young man we taught the gospel over the backyard fence. He was a young man, only twenty-eight years of age, and lived next door to the apartment we were renting.

This man was extremely intelligent—well read, well versed in the current affairs of the world—and an atheist. He felt that if there was a God, as we had explained our conception of God to him, that God would not have created the mess in Christianity that is prevalent in the world today. Therefore, he concluded that there was no God. But he also believed that to be able to communicate with a Supreme Being would be one of the most sublime experiences in the world—an experience which he said he had never felt before, nor did he believe would ever happen.

Spiritually, the Church was not of interest to him, but he enjoyed comparing the doctrines of the Church with other churches, both Christian and non-Christian. As with any new subject that caught his interest, he delved deeply into the subject, reading the *Book of Mormon,* the *Doctrine and Covenants, Pearl of Great Price,* and Talmage's *Jesus the Christ* in just a matter of weeks.

As these "over the backyard" discussions continued, we soon exhausted our resources, without any indication that he was gaining a testimony from his extensive reading, or our discussions. In our frustration at not knowing how to better proceed, we began to encourage the man to pray to gain a spiritual testimony of the gospel, instead of just studying it as a sociological organization. As a result of our persistence, finally one night he said, "I'll put your teachings to a test. I'll pray, and if I receive an answer, I'll join your Church. If not, you can never come back into my home as a minister!"

We agreed to those terms.

My companion and I retired to bed about ten o'clock that night, as we usually did. We were sound asleep when the phone rang. I was a little groggy as I answered the phone, and on the other end was our next door neighbor, obviously very excited.

"Elders! Come over, quick!" he said. "I've got to see you. Right now!"

"It's late," I mumbled. "It's one o'clock in the morning!"

"I know it's late, but I've got to talk to you. Come quick!"

So we quickly dressed and went to his home to find him sitting on the sofa, shaking, obviously very upset, and very white. He exclaimed very excitedly, "Elders, I've got to be baptized! Tonight!"

We looked at our watches and said, "It's only a little after one o'clock in the morning. The water would be cold. Besides, the chapel is locked."

"I don't care! I'll go get baptized in the river! We've got to do it right now!"

"Well, what happened?" we asked.

"Elders," he said, "something wonderful happened tonight! I suppose the most wonderful thing I've ever experienced. I was able to communicate with a source higher than myself. A Supreme Being! I *do* believe in God, Elders! In fact," he said, "I *know* there's a God!"

He then went on to relate what had happened to him that night. He had waited until his family had gone to bed that evening to fulfill the commitment that he had made to us to test prayer, and see if it really did work; to find out if there really was a Father in heaven and to put the Book of Mormon and the truthfulness of the gospel to the test.

He prayed as we had told him to, although very mechanically. When he got up after having not felt anything, he said to himself, "Well, that's just what I expected—nothing!"

But, as he sat there thinking about that prayer, he said, "I thought to myself that *if* there was a God, as the elders told me there was, he probably would not have answered that prayer because of the wrong motives that I had. I was doing this purely for an intellectual exercise. I was just curious about this knowledge merely from a worldly standpoint."

He then began to wonder what would happen if he promised God, *if* there was a God, that he would join his Church and serve him and build up his kingdom on earth, if he would only communicate with him and tell him the truthfulness of the Book of Mormon.

So this young man again knelt down by the side of his bed, and prayed with a different intent. And as he started to pray, the Spirit of the Lord came upon him to such an extent that, as he reached out to touch his wife to awaken her, he found that he could not, as he was paralyzed. He could not move.

Then his eyes were opened, and a vision of the story of the Book of Mormon was unfolded to him. He saw Joseph receiving the "Golden Plates," the translation of the Book of Mormon, and the apostles giving Joseph Smith and Oliver Cowdery the priesthood.

After the vision left him, he immediately called my companion and me requesting, almost demanding, baptism into the Lord's Church. The Lord had honored his sincere request for a knowledge of the truth, and now he was determined to keep his commitment to that Supreme Being.

This man is now the branch president in his small community, having been truly converted by the communication that he experienced that night with our Father in heaven.

Workings of the Spirit

Benbow Farm

WILFORD WOODRUFF

March 1st, 1840, was my birthday, when I was thirty-three years of age. It being Sunday, I preached twice through the day to a large assembly in the City Hall, in the town of Hanley, and administered the sacrament unto the Saints.

In the evening I again met with a large assembly of the Saints and strangers, and while singing the first hymn the Spirit of the Lord rested upon me, and the voice of God said to me, "This is the last meeting that you will hold with this people for many days."

I was astonished at this, as I had many appointments out in that district.

When I arose to speak to the people, I told them that it was the last meeting I should hold with them for many days. They were as much astonished as I was.

At the close of the meeting four persons came forward for baptism, and we went down into the water and baptized them.

In the morning I went in secret before the Lord, and asked Him what His will was concerning me.

The answer I got was, that I should go to the south, for the Lord had a great work for me to perform there, as many souls were waiting for the word of the Lord.

On the 3rd of March, 1840, in fulfillment of the word of the Lord to me, I took coach and road to Wolverhampton, twenty-six miles, and spent the night there.

On the morning of the 4th I again took coach, and rode through Dudley, Stourbridge, Stourport and Worcester, and then walked a number of miles to Mr. John Benbow's, Hill Farm, Castle

Frome, Ledbury, Herefordshire. This was a farming country in the south of England, a region where no Elder of the Latter-day Saints had visited.

I found Mr. Benbow to be a wealthy farmer, cultivating three hundred acres of land, occupying a good mansion, and having plenty of means. His wife, Jane, had no children.

I presented myself to him as a missionary from America, an Elder of the Church of Jesus Christ of Latter-day Saints, who had been sent to him by the commandment of God as a messenger of salvation, to preach the gospel of life unto him and his household, and the inhabitants of the land.

Mr. Benbow and his wife received me with glad hearts and thanksgiving. It was in the evening when I arrived, having traveled forty-eight miles by coach and on foot during the day, but after receiving refreshments we sat down together, and conversed until two o'clock in the morning.

Mr. Benbow and his wife rejoiced greatly at the glad tidings which I brought unto them of the fullness of the everlasting gospel, which God had revealed through the mouth of His Prophet, Joseph Smith, in these last days.

I rejoiced greatly at the news that Mr. Benbow gave me, that there was a company of men and women—over six hundred in number—who had broken off from the Wesleyan Methodists, and taken the name of United Brethren. They had forty-five preachers among them, and had chapels and many houses that were licensed according to the law of the land for preaching in.

This body of United Brethren were searching for light and truth, but had gone as far as they could, and were continually calling upon the Lord to open the way before them, and send them light and knowledge that they might know the true way to be saved.

When I heard these things I could clearly see why the Lord had commanded me, while in the town of Hanley, to leave that place of labor and go to the south, for in Herefordshire there was a great harvest-field for gathering many Saints into the kingdom of God.

I retired to my bed with joy after offering my prayers and thanksgiving to God, and slept sweetly until the rising of the sun.

I arose on the morning of the 5th, took breakfast, and told Mr. Benbow I would like to commence my Master's business, by preaching the gospel to the people.

He had a large hall in his mansion which was licensed for preaching, and he sent word through the neighborhood that an American missionary would preach at his house that evening.

As the time drew nigh many of the neighbors came in, and I preached my first gospel sermon in the house. I also preached on the following evening at the same place, and baptized six persons, including Mr. John Benbow and his wife, and four preachers of the United Brethren.

I spent most of the following day in clearing out a pool of water, and preparing it for baptizing in, as I saw many to be baptized there. I afterwards baptized six hundred in that pool of water. . . .

The whole history of this Herefordshire mission shows the importance of listening to the still small voice of the Spirit of God and the revelations of the Holy Ghost.

The Lord had a people there prepared for the gospel. They were praying for light and truth, and the Lord sent me to them, and I declared the gospel of life and salvation unto them, and some eighteen hundred souls received it, and many of them have been gathered to Zion in these mountains. Many of them have also been called to officiate in the bishopric, and have done much good in Zion. But in all these things we should ever acknowledge the hand of God, and give Him the honor, praise and glory, forever and ever.

℣era's Dream

HOWARD L. BIDDULPH

Vera was one of the early converts in Kiev. Since the time she was a young girl, Vera periodically had a special dream. In the dream she was promised that the true way to God would one day be shown to her and that it would bring her great happiness. At times of great tribulation for her, the dream would come again, assuring her of the Lord's love and the future blessings she would receive if her faith remained strong.

As a young girl during World War II, Vera was separated from her family and held in a work camp in Germany. After the war she was reunited with her mother in Ukraine. In very destitute conditions, Vera nursed her beloved mother until a lingering, painful death of this loved one left Vera alone again.

Vera married, and a daughter was born. Then she cared for her husband in his illness and watched him die, leaving her alone again, this time with a young child to care for. As she grew old, Vera also suffered serious health problems that took her to the brink of death. Yet she was always comforted by the recurring dream that promised a future way of happiness.

Shortly before a very serious operation, in which her life hung in the balance, this aged widow again had her special dream. She was assured that she would survive the operation and be restored to health. Shown the beautiful faces of two fair-haired young men who would soon teach her the true path to God, Vera was promised great happiness and peace if she would accept their message. These were unique, unforgettable faces she saw, unlike any young men she had ever seen in Kiev or Ukraine. She assumed they would be foreigners.

After her recovery, Vera was shopping in downtown Kiev when she recognized with unspeakable joy the faces of two young men dressed in suits and ties—the very faces she had seen in her dream! Like aged Anna in the temple at Jerusalem (see Luke 2:36–38), she had waited throughout her life for the messengers of God.

Elders Aaron Love and Rory Allen were assigned to the area of Kiev where Vera lived, and their own apartment was very close to Vera's home. As a result of meeting them, she received the gospel with joy and was baptized.

In spite of her age, Vera has become a great gospel scholar and a teacher of the Book of Mormon and the Bible. One of my choicest experiences was to attend an Easter Sunday service in her branch and to hear her give one of the truly great sermons I have heard in my lifetime on the Savior Jesus Christ, his suffering and death, his atonement for sin, and his great resurrection. On that sacred occasion, Vera blended movingly the testimonies of Matthew, Mark, Luke, John, and Nephi, as well as her own gentle, loving witness of these events.

Vera lived and saved her widow's mite for the time when she could travel with other members of the Church to the temple of God in Freiberg, Germany, to receive her ordinances and to be sealed to her husband and deceased family. Many years before, she had been sent to that area of Germany as a fearful young girl by the German troops that had occupied her country in World War II. Now, with joy, Vera returned to the same area where she had received her first dream of the gospel, this time to partake of all the ordinances of eternal life.

$\mathscr{A}$ Sermon from a Blank Text

THEODORE B. LEWIS

In the early part of [Jedediah M.] Grant's ministry in [the South], he gained quite a reputation as a ready speaker, frequently responding to invitations to preach from such subjects or texts as might be selected at the time of commencing his sermon, by those inviting him.

In time it became a matter of wonder with many as to how and when he prepared his wonderful sermons. In reply to their queries he informed them that he *never* prepared his sermons as other ministers did. He said, "Of course, I read and store my mind with a knowledge of gospel truths, but I never study up a sermon."

Well, they did not believe he told the truth, for, as they thought, it was impossible for a man to preach such sermons without careful preparation. So, in order to prove it, a number of persons decided to put him to the test, and asked him if he would preach at a certain time and place, and from a text selected by them. They proposed to give him the text on his arrival at the place of meeting, thus giving him no time to prepare.

To gratify them he consented. . . .

The room chosen was in the court house. At the hour appointed the house was packed to its utmost capacity.

Mr. Floyd and a number of lawyers and ministers were present, and occupied front seats.

Elder Grant came in, walked to the stand and opened the meeting as usual. At the close of the second hymn, a clerk, appointed for the occasion, stepped forward and handed a paper (the text) to Elder Grant.

Brother Grant unfolded the paper and found it to be blank. Without any mark of surprise, he held the paper up before the audience, and said:

"My friends, I am here to-day according to agreement, to preach from such a text as these gentlemen might select for me. I have it here in my hand. I don't wish you to become offended at me, for I am under promise to preach from the text selected; and if any one is to blame, you must blame those who selected it. I knew nothing of what text they would choose, but of all texts this is my favorite one.

"You see the paper is blank" (at the same time holding it up to view).

"You sectarians down there believe that out of nothing God created all things, and now you wish me to create a sermon from nothing, for this paper is blank.

"Now, you sectarians believe in a God that has neither body, parts nor passions. Such a God I conceive to be a perfect blank, just as you find my text is.

"You believe in a church without prophets, apostles, evangelists, etc. Such a church would be a perfect blank, as compared with the church of Christ, and this agrees with my text.

"You have located your heaven beyond the bounds of time and space. It exists nowhere, and consequently your heaven is blank, like unto my text."

Thus he went on until he had torn to pieces all the tenets of faith professed by his hearers; and then he proclaimed the principles of the gospel in great power.

He wound up by asking, "Have I stuck to the text, and does that satisfy you?"

As soon as he sat down, Mr. Floyd jumped up and said: "Mr. Grant, if you are not a lawyer, you ought to be one." Then, turning to the people, he added: "Gentlemen, you have listened to a wonderful discourse, and with amazement. Now, take a look at Mr. Grant's clothes. Look at his coat! his elbows are almost out; and his knees are almost through his pants. Let us take up a collection."

As he sat down, another eminent lawyer, Joseph Stras, Esq., still living in Jeffersonville, arose and said:

"I am good for one sleeve in a coat and one leg in a pair of pants, for Mr. Grant."

The presiding elder of the M. E. church, South, was requested to pass the hat around, but replied that he would not take up a collection for a "Mormon" preacher.

"Yes you will!" said Mr. Floyd.

"Pass it around!" said Mr. Stras, and the cry was taken up and repeated by the audience, until, for the sake of peace, the minister had to yield. He accordingly marched around with a hat in his hand, receiving contributions, which resulted in a collection sufficient to purchase a fine suit of clothes, a horse, saddle and bridle for Brother Grant, and not one contributor a member of the Church of Jesus Christ of Latter-day Saints, though some joined subsequently. And this from a sermon produced from a blank text.

"*I* Had Never Preached in My Life"

CLAUDIUS V. SPENCER

I went aboard a New York steamer and applied for a ticket for passage and state room to that city [en route to my mission in England]. . . . On this same day I had the "blues" as I hope never to have them again. I had nearly concluded that there could not be either sense or inspiration in the authorities of the Church sending me to England on a mission, and, that when I got to New York City I would go over to my native town where I had some property and quietly settle among friends and relatives. So great was the power that the devil had over me that when I first stepped in the boat I drew a chair into the niche by the "figure head" to avoid having conversation with anyone. I had sat there but a few moments when a person came up behind me and remarked that it was a pleasant evening. I made no reply.

"Boat making fine time," said he.

Still I did not answer. Soon he spoke again: "Are you traveling far, young man?"

I jerked my chair around and answered very spitefully, "I have *come* a long way and I am *going* a long way, all the way from Salt Lake to England. Is there anything else you want?" My abruptness had sent him back several feet, and he was looking at me with about as much curiosity as if he were viewing a wild animal.

Very soon he smiled and said, "Yes, if you come from Salt Lake there is a good deal more I want."

He commenced asking questions, and soon several more persons gathered around; but just then the dinner bell rang, and they invited me to go to dine, which I did not do, as it seemed to me that I could not have eaten at that time even if it were to save my life. After finishing their repast I was waited upon by three gentlemen, who stated they had engaged the cabin from the captain and wished me to preach. I told them I had never preached in my life. They wanted to know for what I was going to England. I told them to preach. They then wanted to know why I would not preach in the cabin, my answer being that it was because I was not sent here to preach. We finally compromised the matter by my consenting to go to the cabin and answer questions. The room was so crowded that they could not sit down, but stood around in circles and took turns in asking me questions.

When I first sat down I noticed a large, black-eyed, black-haired man, and said to myself, "When he comes I will have the devil." After some time he pushed forward and literally covered me with compliments. He then remarked, "You must excuse me, young friend, after your testimony of the goodness of your people, for asking why such men as George J. Adams, John C. Bennett, Dr. Foster, Charles Foster and others could not live peaceably in your community?"

My answer followed like lightning: "It was because they were such gamblers, whore-masters, black-legs and rascals as you are."

He made a bound for me; six men caught him, pulled him to the outside of the circle, and slapping him on the back told him with an oath, that if God Almighty had come down out of heaven, He could not have told his character any better than the little "Mormon" had.

I answered questions until about eleven o'clock at night, when I sprang from my chair and said, "Gentlemen, you have had 'Mormonism' enough for one night," and I started for my room. I was stopped and led back to my chair, when I received a unanimous vote of thanks and the proffer to raise me three hundred dollars if I would accept the amount. I told the gentlemen that we preached the gospel without purse or scrip, and that I had already received enough to take me to England. I selected, however, three reliable men, who promised me to see that the three hundred dollars were given to the poor in their neighborhoods during the next winter.

I went into my room and prostrated myself with my face on the floor, and thanked God for the gift of the Holy Ghost, for I had most surely talked by inspiration. I asked forgiveness for my unbelief, and from that time I was wholly contented to go to England.

"The Gain and the Joy
Are All Mine"

MARION D. HANKS

One night a fine young missionary came to the mission home with anxiety written all over his face. I knew there was trouble, and I stood to meet it. He could hardly speak through his excitement and his sorrow. He said, "Elder Christensen has been hit on his bicycle—hit by a car—and he is in the hospital in the emergency ward." We rushed to the hospital. A rather flippant little nurse was at the desk. I said: "I am President Hanks. I am the legal guardian of James Christensen, who was hit by an automobile. Can you tell me where he is?"

She said, "In the morgue!" From the look on my face she became a bit ashamed, recoiled, and said, "Oh, I'm sorry, didn't you know?"

I said, "No. I did not know."

"He was dead on arrival," she responded. . . .

The day came in England when we were to prepare our companion to send him home to his good mother, who lives here in Salt Lake. She had no husband. This was her only son, and she had a younger daughter.

My heart was filled with sorrow as I went to the mortuary to dress our companion in his temple clothing. I took with me three missionaries. . . .

When the four of us reached the funeral home I went inside with the mortician. He and I did some preliminary things, and then I went back outside and said to my three young companions: "I would like to invite you to come in and help me put the temple clothing on Elder Christensen, if you would like to come. If you feel at all uncomfortable or uneasy, if you don't want to come, that is perfectly all right; I understand fully. In that case, just wait for me here. But if you would like to come in with me I think it will be a great experience for you." All three of them came in.

The funeral director was a giant of a man who was nationally known. He had performed funeral services for the king of England, who had died some years before. He had served at many, many funerals. His business, and he was tender at it, was taking care of those who had passed on. He stood by while these three missionaries and I tenderly, lovingly put on our companion the special clothing worn in a temple and by those being buried who have received the endowment. . . .

I watched these three missionaries with as much tenderness of feeling as I have ever watched anything in my life. I felt so full of it myself. . . . There was a spirit in that room such as I had never felt before, a particular spirit for that particular setting. I watched these strong, rugged young men, who loved this missionary, walk around him, adjust his clothing; then they would reach out and pat him just a little, just a touch. You see, we all knew something very, very well. We *knew* it. Jim Christensen wasn't really there, not in that form we could see. We were doing for him and his mom and sister the last sweet, brotherly thing we could do in England; but we knew—and our hearts were swelled with joy at this knowledge—that the "real" Jim Christensen wasn't lying before us. We thought he was with us, all right, and this was no spectacular thing—there was no vision, no voice. Just the strongest kind of assurance I have ever felt in all my life.

When we had finished our preparations I said to the funeral director: "We would like to kneel in prayer here. Would you like to join us?" He said, "I would be honored." And so we knelt, and I talked to the Lord. When we stood up the room was filled with the sweetest peace I have ever known.

When we had left the room the director said to me: "President Hanks, I have never known Mormons before. This is the first Mormon funeral I have had anything to do with, the first death of any Mormon I have attended. I have misunderstood. I have heard a lot of things about you people and I have misunderstood. Just let me tell you, please, that for the rest of my life I'll not forget what I felt in that room today, and you can count on it. I will do everything I can do to correct the misapprehensions that are bandied about in this land about you folks."

I suppose it really needn't be said, but I will just say it because it is so: he didn't charge for his services in that case. He wrote me a little note in which he said: "The gain and the joy are all mine."

A Living Testimony

MELVIN S. TAGG

During the period of tenseness preceding the outbreak of the Samoan civil war, a native, crawling on his hands and knees to show respect, approached Elder Edward J. Wood and his companion, Joseph H. Dean. Through an interpreter, the native told of a lady on another island who wanted the missionaries to come and heal her sick child. He said the lady had seen these two elders in a dream, and he asked them to follow him quickly. The elders wanted to be helpful to the lady, but because of the native law restricting the activity of Mormon missionaries and because of the war, they knew not what to do. The native Saints warned the elders that harm would come of it, that it was only a trap to ensnare the servants of the Lord. The elders tried to anticipate the result of a successful healing and an unsuccessful healing. In their dilemma, they went to a secluded spot under a banyan tree and there inquired of the Lord as to whether it would be right to undertake this mission of mercy. Elder Wood said that while they were in the attitude of prayer he heard a voice telling him "it was alright to go to the other island." This was the assurance the elders needed and they were soon on their way across the three-mile stretch of ocean that separated the two islands. Despite a stormy sea, they reached their destination in safety. The mother, who had been waiting on the beach for them, greeted them respectfully and motioned for them to follow her to her house. Addressing the elders the woman remarked, "I am glad that you have come. It is alright. Here is my child." Whereupon, she lifted a white sheet from off the body of the child who was lying on the floor of the hut. The elders declared the child to be dead, but the mother insisted otherwise and added, "You do what I saw you do last night in my dream, and she will be well." The faith of the elders was at a low ebb, and knowing the natives to be extremely superstitious, they feared the consequences "should they administer to the afflicted one without the desired results." While the elders were thus meditating, the mother submitted this question to them, "Have you the authority to do what I saw you do in my dream? You anointed that child with oil; you laid your hands upon her head." No longer could they hesitate. They were convinced they had the authority so they administered to the child. After completing the ordinance they covered the child with the cloth and took their departure.

Nothing more was heard of the child or its mother until about two years later when Elder Wood was called to labor on yet another island. Much to his surprise he was greeted on the beach by half-clad natives running back and forth and swinging long knives. He was soon entirely surrounded by them, but before long he was greeted kindly by a woman who called him by name. "I do not know you," he replied as he stepped back from her. Reminding Elder Wood that he did know her, she called to her side a young child about nine years old and, addressing the crowd, she said: "This is a living testimony of the great power of the gospel, and the power and authority held by Mr. Wood and his associates. They administered to this child over two years ago. I have never seen them since, but I know they have the power of God with them, and all of you must listen to their message" (quoted in Thomas C. Romney, "Edward J. Wood," *The Gospel in Action* [Salt Lake City: Deseret News Press, 1949], p. 262).

Then, addressing Elder Wood, she said that she was the daughter of the high chief of the island and that he could stay at her home and his needs would be supplied. The group then proceeded to her father's house, where Elder Wood spent nearly all night preaching to them with great power. The good woman, daughter of the chief, told him that she had been praying earnestly for Mormon missionaries to be sent to her home, where, she felt, there would be great good accomplished in the spreading of the gospel.

"𝒥 Was Truly Astonished"

SUSAN EASTON BLACK

In the summer of 1835, two Mormon Elders preached in Lookinglass Prairie, Illinois. They told of a modern prophet on the earth and his translation of an ancient scripture. Listening to their sermons were seventeen-year-old Sarah Pea and her father. When the Elders completed their sermons, they were invited by Sarah's father to dine with the Pea family. Sarah related:

> After supper was over a number of neighbors gathered, to hear these strange men talk. Feeling anxious to see the Book of Mormon they told us about, I asked one of the elders if I could see the book, and I asked the company to excuse me for the evening. I retired to my room and spent the rest of that evening and most of night reading it. I was truly astonished at its contents. The book left an impression on my mind never to be forgotten. It appeared to be open before my eyes for weeks afterwards. (Quoted in John Henry Evans, *Charles Coulson Rich: Pioneer Builder of the West* [New York: Macmillan, 1936], p. 38.)

The next day when the missionaries left for Ohio, they took with them their copy of the Book of Mormon. Sarah's family believed they would never again see the book or the missionaries.

However, six weeks later Sarah had a dream concerning the missionaries: "I dreamed on Friday night that they would come to our house the next evening, just as the sun was going down, and they would first come in sight at the end of a long lane in front of the house." Sarah was so sure of her dream that she asked her father to come home early that afternoon from a neighboring town. Her father asked, "Why are you so particular? Is your young man coming?" To his teasing, Sarah responded, "No, father, but those two Mormon elders will be here to-night." Her father asked if she had received word from them. Sarah replied, "No, but I dreamed last night they would be here, and I feel sure it will be so." Sarah later explained:

> Father said I must be crazy, for those men were hundreds of miles away. But I insisted: "Father, hurry home this evening, for I am sure they will come." He only laughed, and he and mother went off to town. Then I said to my sister, "Let's prepare, for those men will surely be here." (Quoted in Evans, p. 39.)

Just as the sun was setting, the missionaries arrived at Sarah's home. As Sarah explained her dream that anticipated their coming, the missionaries told her, "We had a dream that we were to return here and baptize you and build up a church in this region." She asked the Elders to sit inside the house, then returned to the porch to wait for her parents. She related:

> In a very short time my father and mother drove into the yard. As I was standing on the porch, my father said to me, "Well, Sarah, where are your Mormon elders?" I told him they were in the house, at the same time they stepped out on the porch, to meet him. Father was struck with astonishment. (Quoted in Evans, pp. 39–40.)

The Elders stayed that night with the family and again discussed the coming forth of the Book of Mormon. They remained in the area until they had built up a congregation of over seventy members, including Sarah, her father, her mother, and her sister.

He Was Speaking Words Which He Did Not Understand

ANTHON H. LUND

The writer recollects hearing the late Elder George G. Bywater relate an incident in his experience while upon his first mission. He was laboring in Wales in company with another Elder of more experience than himself. The senior Elder generally did most of the preaching. Upon one occasion the latter took a severe cold on his lungs and became so hoarse that he could scarcely whisper. An appointment had been made for him to preach at a certain place where the congregation would be mostly composed of Welsh-speaking people. The experienced missionary was unable to speak on account of his hoarseness, so he informed his young companion that he would have to do the speaking. Elder Bywater felt his weakness and inability to satisfy the people's expectations, as he did not understand the Welsh language; but, on being requested to do so, he arose to address the audience as best he could, depending upon the Spirit of the Lord to assist him in his utterances. He began by speaking in the English tongue— the only one he understood—but soon he found that he was speaking words which he did not understand, and the fluency with which they came from his lips astonished him. After he had finished preaching his companion, who understood the Welsh tongue, told him that he had delivered an excellent sermon in that language, and that if he lived to the age of Methuselah he would not be able to preach a better one. He had been blessed with the gift of tongues that his hearers might understand the message he had to declare to them.

$\mathcal{F}$ound Twice by the Spirit

HOWARD L. BIDDULPH

Elder Matt Ericson and his companion were fasting and praying that they might be able to fulfill an assignment from their mission president to find and baptize a man suited to be the president of a new branch that would soon be formed in their area. One day they met Sergei for the first time at a bus stop. Returning from a long camping trip, Sergei was unshaven, dirty, and dressed in old clothing. His physical appearance might have deterred the missionaries from making his acquaintance, but Elder Ericson felt a strong impression to approach him and to discuss the restored gospel. Sergei gave the elders his address and invited them to visit him the next day.

Later the elders realized that the address Sergei had given them was incomplete. Unable to locate him, they reluctantly went on with their other work. Sergei waited in vain for the elders to come. He was disappointed that they had missed the appointment. When he realized that he may have given them an incorrect or incomplete address, Sergei felt a strange urgency to search for the two strangers. It seemed unlikely that in a city of several million people he could find them again, but he spent several hours trying.

Several days later the missionaries passed the same bus stop again and were frantically hailed by a well-groomed, impressive looking man who appeared to know them. He introduced himself as Sergei, the man with whom they had made the previous appointment. Given Sergei's recent haircut and shave and the fact that he was suitably dressed for his profession as an executive, the missionaries never would have recognized him.

The missionaries met with Sergei, his wife, Valya, who is a professional teacher and linguist, and their children. Soon all were baptized. Two months later Sergei was called to preside over a branch being organized in that part of the city. Valya became an outstanding seminary teacher and translator of curriculum materials for the Church.

Sergei felt a persistent impression to invite his brother, Alexei, along with Alexei's wife and children, to visit him and hear the gospel. Sergei delayed acting on the impression because he was sure Alexei had no interest in religion and also because he lived a great distance away. When Sergei did invite the family for a visit, great blessings resulted: the family accepted the gospel, were all baptized, and became the first Latter-day Saints in their entire area of the country.

Upon being introduced to Alexei, the impression came to me that he, like Sergei, would one day become a fine Church leader. When the city where Sergei's family lived was finally opened, Alexei was called to be president of the first branch of the Church organized there. Both brothers and their families have since received their eternal temple blessings.

Elder Ericson and Sergei have often expressed their gratitude to the Lord for bringing them together, not once, but twice, so that an extended, elect family could accept the gospel of Jesus Christ and the Church in Ukraine could receive strong leadership for two cities.

My Brother's Conversion

HEBER J. GRANT

As I stand here today, I remember what to me was the greatest of all the great incidents in my life, in this tabernacle. I saw for the first time, in the audience, my brother who had been careless, indifferent and wayward, who had evinced no interest in the gospel of Jesus Christ, and, as I saw him for the first time in this building, and as I realized that he was seeking God for light and knowledge regarding the divinity of this work, I bowed my head and I prayed God that if I were requested to address the audience, that the Lord would inspire me by the revelations of his Spirit, by that Holy Spirit in whom every true Latter-day Saint believes, that my brother would have to acknowledge to me that I had spoken beyond my natural ability, that I had been inspired of the Lord. I realized that if he made that confession, then I should be able to point out to him that God had given him a testimony of the divinity of this work. Brother Milton Bennion was sitting on the stand that day, and he had been asked to address the congregation. President Angus M. Cannon came to me and said, "Before you entered the building, Brother Grant, I had invited Brother Milton Bennion to speak, but he can come some other day."

I said, "Let him speak." Brother Cannon said, "Well, I will ask him to speak briefly, and you will please follow him."

Brother Bennion told of his visit around the world; among other things, of visiting the sepulchre of Jesus.

I took out of my pocket a book that I always carried, called a *Ready Reference,* and I laid it down on the stand in front of me, when I stood up to speak. . . .

. . . I prayed for the inspiration of the Lord, and the faith of the Latter-day Saints, and I never thought of the book from that minute until I sat down, at the end of a thirty-minute address. I closed my remarks at 12 minutes after 3 o'clock, expecting that President George Q. Cannon would follow me. Brother Angus came to the upper stand, and said, "George, please occupy the balance of the time."

He said, "No, I do not wish to speak," but Brother Angus refused to take "No" for an answer.

Brother Cannon said, finally: "Alright, go take your seat, and I will say something," and he arose and said in substance: "There are times when the Lord Almighty inspires some speaker by the revelations of his Spirit, and he is so abundantly blessed by the inspiration of the living God that it is a mistake for anybody else to speak following him, and one of those occasions has been today, and I desire that this meeting be dismissed without further remarks," and he sat down.

I devoted the thirty minutes of my speech almost exclusively to a testimony of my knowledge that God lives, that Jesus is the Christ, and to the wonderful and marvelous labors of the Prophet Joseph Smith, and bearing witness to the knowledge God had given me that Joseph was in very deed a prophet of the true and living God.

The next morning my brother came into my office and said, "Heber, I was at meeting yesterday and heard you preach."

I said, "The first time you ever heard your brother preach, I guess?"

"Oh, no," he said, "I have heard you lots of times."

I said, "I never saw you in meeting before."

"No," he said, "I generally come in late and go into the gallery. I often go out before the meeting is over. But you never spoke as you did yesterday. You spoke beyond your natural ability. You were inspired of the Lord." The identical words I had uttered the day before, in my prayer to the Lord. . . .

I said to him, "Are you still praying for a testimony of the gospel?"

He said, "Yes, and I am going nearly wild."

I asked, "What did I preach about yesterday?"

He replied, "You know what you preached about."

I said, "Well, you tell me."

"You preached upon the divine mission of the Prophet Joseph Smith."

I answered, "And I was inspired beyond my natural ability; and I never spoke before—at any time you have heard me, as I spoke yesterday. Do you expect the Lord to get a club and knock you down? What more testimony do you want of the gospel of Jesus Christ than that a man speaks beyond his natural ability and under the inspiration of God, when he testifies of the divine mission of the prophet Joseph?" The next Sabbath he applied to me for baptism.

Conversion and Testimony

A Remarkable Conversion

LEGRAND RICHARDS

While filling a mission in Holland from 1905 to 1908, the following experience was related to me by a member of the Rotterdam Branch. He indicated that he had formerly been a minister of the Gospel, and that he had had a church congregation of his own in Rotterdam. At that time he was a man around sixty, with a splendid personality, a grey beard, and imposing in appearance. The missionaries had converted quite a number of his congregation and these good Saints loved this minister so much that they pled with him to investigate Mormonism. Finally they persuaded him to attend one of our meetings in Rotterdam. At the close of the meeting, the missionaries engaged him in conversation at the door, and he denounced Joseph Smith as a false prophet, as an imposter, and everything vile he could think of. He then left and returned home. He said he did not know what he had done, but he had displeased God because when he retired to bed he could not sleep. He tossed from one side to the other, until the early morning hours when he arose and walked the streets until he thought the missionaries would be up, and then he presented himself at the mission office and asked the privilege to borrow a copy of the Book of Mormon.

It has been my privilege to speak in the same meeting with this man upon many occasions, and to visit homes of investigators. I have never had a finer missionary companion, and I have thrilled over and over again as I have heard him stand and with all the fervor and sincerity that a man could possess, testify that he knew that Joseph Smith was a prophet of God and the Book of Mormon was true.

"That Is Why
I Joined the Church"

KENNETH W. GODFREY

While serving as a mission president in Pennsylvania I was asked to speak at the Pittsburgh Theological Seminary. I took my assistants with me. As I addressed those men who were about to become ministers in a variety of Protestant churches, the impression came to me that they believed the only reason I was a Mormon was because I had been born and raised in my church. When I told them my impression, several smiled and nodded their heads. I said, "That is not the reason I am a Latter-day Saint, but instead of my telling you the real reason I am a Mormon, I am going to ask my assistant, Elder Zeller, to tell you why he joined the Church. He is the only member of his family that belongs to the LDS Church and he joined when he was about seventeen or eighteen years old. Furthermore, he is bright enough to be accepted at any university in the country, including Harvard, Yale, Princeton, Brown, or even the University of Pittsburgh."

Elder Zeller almost fell off his chair, having had no warning that he would address that group. But, being obedient, he did as I asked. After relating a few things about his life and his search for the true church, he began to recite Joseph Smith's account of his First Vision, word for word, as he had memorized it. He came to the words, "I saw two Personages, whose brightness and glory defy all description, standing above me in the air. One of them spake unto me, calling me by name and said, pointing to the other—This is My Beloved Son. Hear Him!" (JS—H 1:17). The spirit of the Lord filled the room, bearing witness that Elder Zeller spoke the truth. Some eyes began to tear. Then Elder Zeller said, "That is why I joined the Church, because God the Father and

Jesus Christ appeared to Joseph Smith and later through him restored the true church to the earth."

After Elder Zeller concluded his testimony I said, "That is why I am a Mormon, too. It makes little difference that my great-great-grandfather was converted as a grown man, that my great-grandfather was a Mormon, my grandfather and my father, too. I am a Latter-day Saint because, like Elder Zeller, I know that Joseph Smith was a prophet."

The Road to Sharon

ALBERT C. COOPER

Even after all these years, I can still close my eyes and see the small dust cloud following the noisy rattle-trap Ford which struggled toward us that summer afternoon. I can vividly recall the two young men with out-of-place hats squared on crew cut heads who introduced themselves as Elder Dale Pope and Elder Jim Lillywhite. To say that their visit was a surprise would be gratuitous folklore: I had, in a sense, asked for it. The "chance" meeting had really had its origin in events which started the previous fall.

When the letter arrived from Whitefield, New Hampshire, announcing that my older brother Frank and his wife, Sybil, had recently been baptized at a place called Sharon and were now members of The Church of Jesus Christ of Latter-day Saints (commonly called Mormons), I was, like my other two brothers, shocked. While I knew almost nothing about Mormons, I felt somehow betrayed that a brother I had always regarded as sensible to a fault should have fallen prey to some obscure sect. Only later would we learn that Frank, raised an Episcopalian like the rest of us, and his strict Catholic wife had been engaged in a serious search for a church they could both feel comfortable in at the time two young elders, lost amid the maze of country dirt roads, had knocked on the door of their New Hampshire home. . . .

On one of those weekend reunions at the family's homeplace near Randolph, Vermont, the first in a series of debates pitted Frank and Sybil against the rest of us. They had had the temerity to bring their two elders with them, adding to the animosity which had grown between us. It must not have been a happy experience for the two missionaries, who suddenly found themselves in the midst of four brothers who had grown up together in an atmosphere where discussion and debate around the Sunday dinner table had been the high point of every week.

The only small victory which went to "the enemy" that day occurred when Frank managed to slip complementary copies of a black-covered book into the hands of each of us as we parted. I can recall not knowing what to do with that copy of the Book of Mormon when we arrived home. It didn't seem right just to throw it away. I had been taught from an early age to revere books. In our family, even *Collier's* magazines were kept, in yellowing boxes, long after any possible usefulness had passed. So I slipped the book behind other, less offending titles on my bookshelf. I had no plans to look inside, and I didn't want the embarrassment of explaining its presence to visiting friends.

I was twenty-five years old when this intrusion in my life began. I was an "old" twenty-five. Shirley and I had been married for four years; we had a small child and a second on the way. Behind me lay four long years of military service and the kind of real-world education which builds a healthy cynicism. I had been to Korea; I had "seen the Elephant" as the veterans of an earlier war would have said. I had tried the religious faith of my fathers and found it wanting. I firmly believed the Bible to be a collection of well-worn and loosely linked fables, designed to encourage people to live together in some kind of harmony. I had seen nothing to indicate that it was anything more than that.

Shirley and I had been married conventionally in a Congregational church because it was what young people like us were supposed to do. The families expected it. We held no particular church preference, notwithstanding the anti-Catholic prejudice of our family roots. I was engrossed in a business career and a social life which were comfortable and satisfying. I had developed an appreciation of fine old wines, and took pride in the dark beer I brewed myself in ten-gallon batches from an old recipe passed on to me from a grizzled prohibitionist I met in Washington state. My collection of pipes totaled twenty-six, as I recall, gathered from all over the world, and I fancied myself a thoughtful, studious, well-read sophisticate, puffing amiably and disarmingly on my hand-carved Schoenleber. . . .

All told, I was living a life I enjoyed. I was accepted among peers I admired and whose company I found stimulating. In my firm I was definitely on the way up. . . .

During those summer months we regularly had contact with Frank and Sybil at family get-togethers. Curious changes were taking place in these two. Frank—always the quiet, almost reclusive brother—had become talkative and outgoing, never missing a chance to "preach to others." And Sybil, the shy, awkward farm-girl with no musical talent at all, had become a branch chorister, and somehow managed to pass out Mormon songbooks and get us singing in the family livingroom.

More and more I found myself impressed with the logic of Frank's religious arguments, and a grudging admiration began to take hidden shape—hidden because I was expected to carry the debating flag for the rest of us. After all, I had overheard our father telling Mom, "Well, we don't have to worry about Al falling for that bunk. He's the one with a head on his shoulders."

One rainy afternoon when I found myself home alone, my growing curiosity led me to retrieve the black book from its hiding place. Wedged between the opening pages was a tract entitled *The Joseph Smith Story,* and I read it first before starting into the book itself. On succeeding occasions, when I was sure Shirley wouldn't observe me doing so, I continued my surreptitious study, until one day I somehow discovered that she was doing the same thing when I wasn't around.

After that, we sat down together and began reading aloud from page one. We were well into Second Nephi when our elders arrived on the scene, sent no doubt by my brother Frank, who had sensed that we were ready.

My resistance to "recruitment" was deep-seated, and I had no intention of allowing these smooth-faced young zealots to convert me. I read and studied in self-defense as well as from curiosity. Fawn Brodie and every anti-Mormon author I could find fueled my search. I eagerly anticipated each lesson from the elders, bait-ing them with every extraneous question I could think of. I knew just enough about their upcoming discussion to be dangerous. While I knew the Book of Mormon was true, and had for some time, I still did not want to join anything: intellectually I was con-verted, but a spiritual awakening had not taken place and might not.

By now, Elder Pope had been replaced by a fast-talking Californian named Raymond Lane. Elder Lillywhite had become kind of a family member to us, although he was, in my estima-tion, totally unimpressive as a teacher. He had great difficulty in delivering a discussion, and was frequently stumped for words and obviously ill at ease. It was a game for me to make mince-meat of his inarticulate attempts to deal with my questions. It was on such an evening that he finally surrendered. The room was filled with dense blue smoke from the rum-dipped Crooks I saved for such occasions, just to let them know they weren't getting any-where with me.

Filled with frustration, Jim Lillywhite closed his notebook and gave in. "I'm sorry, Brother Cooper. I can't answer all your ques-tions," he stammered. "You're too smart for me."

Then he reached for his Book of Mormon—it was all he had left. Eyes brimming with tears, he held the book in his shaking hands and bore his testimony from his heart. It was all he had left. But it was enough.

After the elders left that night, Shirley and I sat talking.

"Don't you think," she said, "it's about time you allowed those young men to tell us the things they have come all this way to share? Don't you think it's about time you stopped playing your games?"

The next day I had a ritualistic bonfire in my backyard. I burned my twenty-six pipes and my rum-dipped Crooks, and in the smoke of the blaze I acknowledged that I had changed. I was no longer, and never again could be, the same person. I poured the last bottle of Spanish sherry down the drain, and threw out my box of Lipton tea. In time I would even bring myself—

somewhat ludicrously with the help of the two missionaries—to uncap and pour out the last of my best-ever batch of home brew.

On a rainy and gray Saturday in September of 1958, Shirley and I were baptized in Sharon, Windsor County, Vermont, a few hundred yards from a crumbling stone wall marking the place where the modern-day prophet Joseph Smith was born. After Elder Jim Lillywhite and Elder Raymond Lane led us into the font, my brother Frank, who had been ordained an elder the previous week, confirmed me and my younger brother (to whom I had led the elders) members of The Church of Jesus Christ of Latter-day Saints.

As a result of our conversion forty-two members of the extended Cooper family, living in five states, are now active members of the Church. Their sons have served missions, and they themselves are responsible for the conversions of hundreds of others. Our genealogy and temple work reaches back many generations and continues at a steady pace. It has been my privilege to serve as branch president, seminary instructor, stake missionary, high councilor, and in many other Church positions.

Like a Little Child

MARION D. HANKS

I thought of a day when a man who had spent more than half a century in the ministry came to Salt Lake, after having met two of our missionaries in California, to find out if all the members of the Church had what he had felt in these two humble young men. . . . They had not been able to reach him with scripture or reason. He had the degrees, the experience, half a century in the pulpit. But they had reached him through a spirit he could not fail to feel and could not explain.

We had a long talk which I cannot share with you, but the heart of which came when I said to him: "Doctor, there is just one question I need to ask you. Have you been baptized by an authorized administrator for the remission of your sins?" He got a hurt look in his eye. He said, "Elder Hanks, after this wonderful experience of brotherhood and the feeling we've had together, are you telling me that you think I have to go down in a pond of water like a little child to make some kind of a covenant with God?"

I opened this book and began to read from Matthew chapter three, words with which you are very familiar: "And Jesus answering said unto him, Suffer it to be so now: for thus it becometh us to fulfill all righteousness. Then he suffered him." (Matthew 3:15.) That is, Jesus was baptized by John.

Now this courteous, gracious, wonderful man almost struck the book from my hand. He said: "I know very well what that says, but nowhere is it explained what it means. Christ was sinless. What does it mean to fulfill all righteousness? Nowhere is it written." And I said, "In this, my beloved friend, you are wrong, because it is, in fact, written." Then I opened . . . to this wonderful Book of Mormon passage, the thirty-first chapter of the second book of Nephi, and read almost verbatim for him the conversation he and I had just had. "Now, if the Lamb of God, he being holy, should have need to be baptized by water, to fulfil all righteousness, O then, how much more need have we, being unholy, to be baptized, yea, even by water!" And then notice:

> And now, I would ask of you, my beloved brethren, wherein the Lamb of God did fulfil all righteousness in being baptized by water?
>
> Know ye not that he was holy? But notwithstanding he being holy, he showeth unto the children of men that, according to the flesh he humbleth himself before the Father, and witnesseth unto the Father that he would be obedient unto him in keeping his commandments. . . .
>
> And again, it showeth unto the children of men the straitness of the path, and the narrowness of the gate, by which they should enter, he having set the example before them.
>
> And he said unto the children of men: Follow thou me. Wherefore, my beloved brethren, can we follow Jesus save we shall be willing to keep the commandments of the Father?
>
> And the Father said: Repent ye, repent ye, and be baptized in the name of my Beloved Son. (2 Nephi 31:5–7, 9–11)

I watched a great, white, wonderful head bow, and a tear hit the carpet. And then I heard the voice, through the tears, say, "Elder Hanks, it appears there are some things we should talk about. Do you have some time?" We sat in an office on Temple Square in Salt Lake City, and I taught him some answers he himself had been seeking for more than fifty years in the pulpit. And after a period of readjustment of his thoughts through the Spirit, he found those two young missionaries in California and went down like a child into the water and was baptized by immersion for the remission of his sins. Then he had hands laid upon his head to receive the gift of the Holy Ghost, received the priesthood, and, at the age of eighty-one, became a noble, reliable, courageous teacher of the gospel.

Reunited by the Gospel

HOWARD L. BIDDULPH

One day in a city [in the Ukraine] an inebriated man at a bus stop wanted to talk with Elder Anthony Brown. This often happened when drunken men and women saw young elders and sisters, and it was rarely productive, so Elder Brown tried to avoid the man. Still the man persisted, and something prompted Elder Brown to talk with him.

Reluctantly Elder Brown made an appointment to meet the man and his family at their apartment. When the elders arrived, this person was drunk again, but he introduced his family and his wife's sister, who was visiting from Riga, Latvia.

The man was not interested in hearing the gospel, but his wife and family and the visiting aunt quickly accepted the teachings of the Church. Then the aunt explained that she had returned to the city to divorce her husband, who remained in Riga, because of the physical abuse she was suffering from his problem with alcohol.

Her acceptance of the gospel made her reconsider her decision to obtain a divorce. She called her husband in Riga and told him of her desire to be baptized into the LDS Church, and of her desire to return and try to work out the problems of their marriage.

Her husband astounded her by relating that he had met the Mormon elders on the street in Riga after her departure. He had believed their message and read the Book of Mormon. And most astounding of all, he had not had a drink since the start of his discussions with the missionaries in Riga. He had been praying that the Lord would soften her heart to forgive him. She did.

The Lord miraculously reunited this couple by bringing each of them to the missionaries, each simultaneously in separate cities. This couple was baptized together and began a new life of reconciliation.

$\mathscr{A}$ Lesson in Humility

ELDRED G. SMITH

A young man told me his experience in becoming a member of the Church, which is typical of many in their activities of investigating the Church. He said the missionaries came to the lesson on the Word of Wisdom. He and his wife were both users of tobacco. After the meeting was over and the missionaries had left, they talked it over with each other and decided between themselves, "Well, if that is what the Lord wants and if this is the Lord's Church, we will try it." He said that he was not particularly concerned about himself, he thought he could do it easily; he was worried about his wife; she had never tried to quit before. On the other hand, he had quit several times. After proving to himself that he could quit, of course, he went back to the use of cigarets again. But he said in this case, it was just the reverse. His wife quit without any apparent difficulty, but he had tremendous difficulty. He became nervous and irritable. He could not rest. He was cranky among his fellow workers. He could not sleep at night. But inasmuch as his wife had quit, he was not going to be outdone by her. So, one night, he became so restless, so disturbed that he could not sleep, and his wife suggested to him that he pray about it. He thought that was a good joke. He ridiculed the idea of prayer; he said, "This is something I have to do. Nobody can help me with this. I can do this." But as the night passed, and he had done everything he could to stimulate sleep and rest without any success, finally in despair he humbled himself enough to kneel at the side of the bed and pray vocally. According to his own testimony, he said that he got up from his prayer, got into bed, went to sleep, and has never been tempted by cigarets since.

He has absolutely lost the taste for tobacco. He said, "The Word of Wisdom was not a health program for me. It was a lesson in humility." He said, "I had to learn humility." That is what it meant to him. As it is with many of the requirements of the Church, we have to demonstrate humble obedience.

First Visit of the Missionaries

JANET CATHERY-KUTCHER

The sun shone that afternoon and so did you
As I opened the door—
Truth standing there and I concerned about my custard
And the kitchen floor.
You spoke, memories stirred and through the
  windows, darkly,
I watched the years
And wondered what it was I longed for
And why my tears.
You went your way, but something lingered in the air,
Peace for my pain;
I picked up my mop, pretended that things could
Be the same again.

$\mathscr{A}$ Testimony of Tithing

LEGRAND RICHARDS

While visiting in Providence, Rhode Island, on April 25, 1926, I remarked to the president of the branch that he must have an outstanding testimony of the law of tithing, since I had noted that he paid a large tithing and paid it so regularly. He replied that he had, and I asked him if he would mind relating the same to me, which he did in about the following manner. He said that his wife and children joined the Church in England some years before. . . . He said that the reason he didn't join the Church was that he did not have faith to pay his tithing and he did not want to be a hypocrite. Some time later when one of the young missionaries was being released to return home, he came to this brother and told him he wanted to baptize him before returning home, to which the brother replied: "You cannot because I haven't the faith to pay my tithing, and I do not want to be a hypocrite." The spirit of the Lord seemed to rest upon the young missionary, and he replied in words something like this, "Brother _____, if you will let me baptize you before I return home, I promise you that within a year from now you will be in America with your family, and will be earning three times as much as you are at the present." The brother said he could not resist availing himself of such a promise, and so he was baptized. He said he could not feel that the promise could come true, as he at the time was under contract to work for the company he was with for an additional two years. It was during the time of World War I when we had such a difficult time to get cloth in this country that would hold its color, and the dye workers of America sent representatives to England to induce some of the dye workers there to come to

America and teach them how to make dyes. Representatives of the American firms called on this man's father, and he indicated that he was not interested, but his son might be. So they approached the son. He said that he could not accept their offer because he was bound to work for his company for an additional two years. They asked if he would be willing to go if they would buy him off so the company would release him from his contract, and he indicated that he would. "Now," he said, "the Lord just threw in a little for good measure. Within a year's time according to the promise of the elder, I was in America with my wife and children, and was earning four times as much as I was when he made me that promise."

$\mathscr{A}$ Spaniard Finds the Truth

KEVIN STOKER

When John Nicholson first met Mileton Gonzales Trejo in July 1874 in Salt Lake City, he was surprised to find the Spaniard didn't look anything like he expected. John anticipated a man with a swarthy complexion, dark hair, piercing black eyes, and a haughty manner. Instead, the Spaniard to whom he was introduced stood a bit below what John considered average height. He was slender and had clear, blue eyes, light hair, and a beard. "His whole makeup was attractive," John later wrote.

The Spaniard struggled to speak English, but his tone of voice was soft and appealing and his story enthralling. Mileton recounted how his father had been a colonel in the Spanish army in the mid 1800s. But the father wanted something better for his son; he urged him to serve God and not the military.

When Mileton was fourteen, his father took him to a convent so he could begin his training for the ministry. But the boy protested and cried, causing his father to relent and take him back home. Five years later, Mileton did follow his father, but this time it was into the Spanish army. Mileton was commissioned as a lieutenant.

During the early part of his military career he met an artillery lieutenant named Barrueco who spoke of a people known as Mormons in the western part of America. Barrueco said the organization of this Mormon church was the same as that in the days of Moses—directed by a prophet to whom God spoke. In time, the officer believed, this church would govern the earth.

Barrueco's words captivated Mileton. He resolved that such a people would be his people and that he would go to them or "die on the road." He requested a transfer to the Philippines, hoping it would be a stepping-stone to the United States. In 1872 he received that transfer, and while passing through France he discovered an LDS pamphlet left by missionaries. What he read shed much more light on this mysterious American religion and increased his desire to go to the Rocky Mountains.

Once in the Philippines, however, Mileton's thoughts of the Mormons and going to the United States were superseded by the pursuit of wealth. Mileton became a successful colonizer and began to have second thoughts about his desires to join the Mormons. He even felt like a traitor to his family and country. Praying for relief from his confusion, he received a soothing sensation and knew the Latter-day Saints were the people of God.

He had to go now. The governor rejected his first application for an eight-month leave, but when that governor was replaced, Mileton reapplied and received approval. In July 1874 he arrived in Salt Lake City where he met a Spanish-speaking French convert named Blanchard. Through Blanchard he became acquainted with John Nicholson, who urged Blanchard to introduce Mileton to President Brigham Young. Mileton met the prophet and was soon baptized. Later he was called on a mission to Mexico and helped establish the LDS colonies there.

But Mileton's greatest contribution to the Lord's work was his knowledge of Spanish. He translated many tracts into Spanish and helped in the translation of the Book of Mormon.

"*I* Would Give Everything I Own if I Could Prove You Wrong"

LUCILE C. TATE

Editor's note: Apostle LeGrand Richards will ever be remembered as a bold and enthusiastic messenger of the restored gospel. His labors in the mission field included a full-time mission to the Netherlands at the age of nineteen and later service as the president of the same mission. The following story is taken from his first mission and is emblematic of the confidence and vigor with which Elder Richards presented the gospel.

He [Elder Richards] lent his own money for fifteen-year-old Arie Sandman to immigrate to America. (It was arranged that when the lad found work there he would repay it, which he later did.) The boy's uncle, Marinus de Rijke, and his wife, a Sandman, allowed missionaries in their home only if they did not discuss religion. When Arie told his uncle of the emigration loan, the older man said, "I would like to meet this man Richards." He came to the boat to bid his nephew farewell, and Arie introduced the two men to each other.

Mr. de Rijke was somewhat pompous and proud, wore a stovepipe hat, carried a walking stick, and smoked a big cigar. At first Elder Richards paid him little attention, but after seeing Arie off, he asked, "Mr. de Rijke, have you ever attended a Mormon meeting?"

"No!" was the emphatic answer.

"Well," Elder Richards said, "the Mormons are cutting enough of a figure in the world that from an educational standpoint it wouldn't hurt you to know a little about them."

He then added, "A man of your learning and experience couldn't be misled."

"Well, I will come," de Rijke said.

The next Sunday he and his wife were at the sacrament meeting. After the meeting, Elder Richards asked him how he had liked the service. He said, "*Tamelijk,*" which means fairly well. Elder Richards then suggested, "I would like to come to your home next week, and you take your Bible and I will take mine, and I will show you things in your Bible you have never read before."

Marinus asked his wife, "What do you say?"

"Oh, let them come," she answered.

The appointment was kept, and they had a "wonderful evening." As the missionaries took their leave, Elder Richards said, "Now, when your minister hears we've been here, he will tell you we are the most wicked people in the world. I suggest you invite him to your home, at any hour of the day or night that meets his convenience, and then invite us also, and you decide which one has the truth." He continued with a paraphrase of John 10:11–13: "He will refuse to come because 'the hireling fleeth when the wolves come, because he is an hireling, but the good shepherd giveth his life for the flock.' You will determine whether he is a hireling."

Mr. de Rijke was the foreman in a distillery, and when the employees left each day he would say to them, "I have had the Mormon missionaries in my home, and my minister will not meet them. If any of you know a minister who is not afraid of Mormons, I would like to get hold of him—I don't care what church he belongs to." Some fine discussions resulted, and after one of them Mr. de Rijke said, "Mr. Richards, I would give everything I own if I could prove you wrong." The young elder laid his little Bible before the man and said, "That is all I ask you to do, and then I will never ask the privilege of coming in your home again."

The man replied, "That is what I have been trying to do, and I have failed."

"I want to thank you for bearing your testimony that you have found the truth," Elder Richards said. "Now what are you going to do about it?"

Shortly after this, Mr. de Rijke and his wife were baptized and immigrated to Utah. Although childless in Holland, they had two children in Utah. The son, Harry, became the "best worker with the Aaronic Priesthood" that Elder Richards ever knew in the Church. The daughter, Nellie, filled three missions.

The Dryland Mormon

FRANKLIN D. RICHARDS

Some time ago, I was in Georgia to dedicate a chapel. As I was walking around in the chapel prior to its dedication, a man came up to me and introduced himself. "I'm a dryland Mormon," he said. I replied, "What do you mean, a dryland Mormon?" He said, "Well, my wife and family are members of the Church, and I come to church quite frequently. I don't smoke or drink, and I have made contributions to the Church, but I've never been baptized." I took him by the lapels, looked him in the eye, and told him there was no such thing as a dryland Mormon.

I said that when Nicodemus came to Christ and asked him what he should do, Christ told him he had to be born again. When Nicodemus could not understand that, the Savior said, "Verily, verily, I say unto thee, Except a man be born of the water and of the Spirit, he cannot enter into the kingdom of God." (John 3:5.)

"And so," I said to this man, "you are denying yourself and your family great blessings by not being baptized. The blessings that await you are, first, a remission of your sins, and second, the receipt of the Holy Ghost."

I continued, "When you have been baptized by water and then have hands laid on your head to receive the Holy Ghost, you will receive a power that will guide and direct your life and will open up the way to greater blessings, such as receiving the priesthood and an opportunity to go into the house of the Lord to receive sealing ordinances that will make your wife and family yours throughout eternity. Now all of these things are dependent upon your being baptized. I would recommend to you that you ask the branch president to interview you to see if you are worthy to be baptized, and if you are worthy, I would recommend that you set your baptism date right away."

After the dedicatory service, people were coming up to talk with me, and this man and his wife came up. Both were in tears as the man shook hands with me and said, "President Richards, I want to be interviewed for baptism." He was interviewed that night by the branch president, was found worthy, and was baptized.

$\mathcal{H}$e Didn't Dare Send Anyone Else

WILFORD WOODRUFF

Editor's note: The following story is taken from Wilford Woodruff's account of his historic mission to England in 1840. His labors were especially successful among a group of Christians called the United Brethren. (For more on Wilford Woodruff's labors among these people, see "Benbow Farm," pp. 57–59.)

On Sunday, the 8th, I preached at Frome's Hill in the morning, at Standley Hill in the afternoon, and at John Benbow's, Hill Farm, in the evening.

The parish church that stood in the neighborhood of Brother Benbow's, presided over by the rector of the parish, was attended during the day by only fifteen persons, while I had a large congregation, estimated to number a thousand, attend my meeting through the day and evening.

When I arose in the evening to speak at Brother Benbow's house, a man entered the door and informed me that he was a constable, and had been sent by the rector of the parish with a warrant to arrest me.

I asked him, "For what crime?"

He said, "For preaching to the people."

I told him that I, as well as the rector, had a license for preaching the gospel to the people, and that if he would take a chair I would wait upon him after meeting.

He took my chair and sat beside me. I preached the first principles of the everlasting gospel for an hour and a quarter. The power of God rested upon me, the Spirit filled the house, and the people were convinced.

At the close of the meeting I opened a door for baptism, and seven offered themselves. Among the number were four preachers and the constable.

The latter arose and said, "Mr. Woodruff, I would like to be baptized."

I told him I would like to baptize him. I went down to the pool and baptized the seven. We then met together and I confirmed thirteen, and broke bread unto the Saints and we all rejoiced together.

The constable went to the rector and told him if he wanted Mr. Woodruff taken up for preaching the gospel, he must go himself and serve the writ, for he had heard him preach the only true gospel sermon he had ever listened to in his life.

The rector did not know what to make of it, so he sent two clerks of the Church of England as spies, to attend our meeting, and find out what we did preach.

But they were both pricked in their hearts and received the word of the Lord gladly, and were baptized and confirmed members of the Church of Jesus Christ of Latter-day Saints.

The rector became alarmed and did not dare to send anybody else.

The ministers and rectors of the South of England called a convention and sent a petition to the Archbishop of Canterbury, to request parliament to pass a law prohibiting the "Mormons" from preaching in the British dominion.

In this petition the rector stated that one "Mormon" missionary had baptized fifteen hundred persons, mostly members of the English church, during the last seven months.

But the archbishop and council, knowing well that the laws of England gave free toleration to all religions under the British flag, sent word to the petitioners that if they had the worth of souls at heart as much as they had the ground where hares, foxes and hounds ran, they would not lose so many of their flock.

I continued to preach and baptize daily.

On the 21st day of March I baptized Elder Thomas Kingston. He was the superintendent of both preachers and members of the United Brethren.

The first thirty days after my arrival in Herefordshire, I had baptized forty-five preachers and one hundred-and-sixty members of the United Brethren, who put into my hands one chapel and forty-five houses, which were licensed according to law to preach in.

This opened a wide field for labor, and enabled me to bring into the Church, through the blessing of God, over eighteen hundred souls during eight months, including all of the six-hundred United Brethren except one person; also including some two hundred preachers of various denominations.

Divine Protection

Evacuation from Germany

DEAN HUGHES AND TOM HUGHES

In August 1939, Hitler began to mass troops along the border of Poland. War was about to begin in Europe. The Church sent out word for all missionaries to leave immediately. Those in eastern Germany were to head to Denmark; those in the western and southern parts of Germany were to escape to Holland.

The nation was in chaos. Trains were being taken over for troops, and telephone lines were jammed. Missionaries were soon on their own, with little chance to communicate with mission leaders.

The missionaries knew they were allowed, by law, to take only ten marks (about two dollars) out of the country. So they bought train tickets and then gave away the rest of their money to members, or bought items they could take with them. That worked fine for those heading to Denmark, and all missionaries from the East German Mission were soon safely out of the country.

Escape into Holland was another matter. Dutch leaders remembered World War I, when they had been unable to feed the thousands of refugees, and thus government officials closed the borders. A few missionaries made it through before the closure, and one sister got across by showing that she had a ticket to travel on to London on a steamer. But most missionaries were stopped.

Without money to buy train tickets, the missionaries couldn't get to any other country. Some managed to get telephone calls through to President M. Douglas Wood of the West German Mission, so he at least knew the problem. But many were stranded, and President Wood had no way to know where all of them were.

That's when miracles began to happen. In Frankfurt, President Wood gave five hundred marks to Elder Norman Seibold. The president told Elder Seibold that thirty-one missionaries were unaccounted for and that he must use his own inspiration to find them, get money or tickets to them, and get them to Denmark. At the same time, President Franklin J. Murdock of the Netherlands Mission received word that six missionaries were stuck just inside the border of Holland. He sent Elder John Kest to find them and to reassure Dutch officials that the missionaries would be sent on to America.

Elder Seibold was a big man. He had played football for the University of Utah. He also proved to be a man of great faith. He had no idea where to find the missionaries, and so he had to follow his own impressions. When he reached Cologne, Germany, after standing up all night on a crowded train, he got off in the huge, crowded station. He climbed on top of a baggage cart and began to whistle "Do What Is Right." He later said it was a bit of a miracle that anyone recognized the song, since he couldn't "carry a tune in a bushel basket." But eight missionaries did recognize the tune and came out of the crowd.

Unfortunately, the tune also attracted a German policeman. He questioned Elder Seibold and then demanded that he turn over his money. But Elder Seibold had *promised* to get the missionaries out. He looked the policeman in the eye and told him that if he tried to take the money, there would be a fight. In Nazi Germany, no one talked that way to the police. Elder Seibold knew that. But he felt he had no choice.

When the policeman demanded that the missionary come with him to a police station, again Elder Seibold said no. He later wrote: "I told him I would go see the military police, but I would not go into the city at all. Why I did that I don't know, but because I was large maybe the Lord made me look larger or something, and I got away with it." Strangely, the military policeman listened. He even agreed to write a letter that allowed Elder Seibold to carry the money and to leave the nation with the missionaries he was trying to find.

For the next three days Elder Seibold searched along the Dutch/German border. In one little town, he saw no reason to get off the train. But a feeling came over him that he must, and so he followed the voice of the Spirit. The little train station was nearly empty, so Elder Seibold walked into the town and then felt impressed to enter a restaurant. He found two elders who had just spent their last pennies for a glass of apple juice. He gave them tickets and money and sent them on their way to Denmark. Then he got back on the train and continued to search.

Meanwhile, Elder Kest arrived in Oldenzaal, Holland, expecting to find at least six missionaries. What he learned was that the elders had been sent back across the border to Bentheim, Germany. Elder Kest had not expected to cross the border, so he hadn't gotten a visa. The missionaries were only a few kilometers away, but he had no way to reach them.

For a few hours he tried making phone calls to government offices. He hoped to get a visa. But all was chaos, and nothing could be done. So Elder Kest, having been instructed to use his best judgment, took a chance. He used all the money he had with him to buy ten tickets to Copenhagen—in case more than six elders were waiting in Bentheim—and then he boarded the train without a visa. For some reason the Dutch authorities did not check his passport, and the train pulled out.

Elder Kest knew he had gotten over the border by a miracle, but in Germany he faced Gestapo officers who did question him about his visa. Then they took him to a room in the station and searched him. They began confiscating everything in his pockets, and he could see they were going to do the same with the train tickets. On impulse, he pulled the tickets out of his pocket and laid them on the table in front of him.

Then another miracle happened. The tickets sat in front of the officers, in plain view, but no one seemed to see them. The officers took everything else Elder Kest had and then told him he could get the items back when he boarded a return train into Holland. At that point, Elder Kest picked up the tickets and put them back in his pocket. "Not an eye flickered," he later reported. Again, the tickets seemed invisible to the officers.

When Elder Kest left the train station, he had forty minutes until he had to reboard and return to Holland. He had no idea where the missionaries were. But someone told him that some Americans had been seen at a hotel in town. Elder Kest hurried to the hotel and found the missionaries. They had used the last of their money to buy some hard rolls and jam. They had prayed constantly for help, and suddenly, like an angel, Elder Kest was there with tickets to Copenhagen. The group knelt together and thanked the Lord, and then Elder Kest ran to catch his train.

The problems were not over, however. Trains were not guaranteed to run on a set schedule. Troops were being rushed to Poland, and passengers with valid tickets were being bumped. For all of the missionaries, not just those in Bentheim, the next couple of days were crazy.

Missionaries boarded any train heading in the direction they needed to go. Sometimes they would get off and try for something else after traveling only a few kilometers. One group reported changing trains seventeen times—and choosing trains by following their inspiration more than by any sort of logic. In another case, a German soldier gave two elders money for train tickets. Two other elders ran across a track in order to board a departing train, and they were arrested. When they complained to a policeman that others were doing the same thing, he turned to look and the elders ran for it. They jumped on the caboose of a moving train with the help of a conductor, who pulled them up.

Elder Seibold made it to Hamburg with several other missionaries, but the group could find no space on any train. Finally they were allowed, for reasons they didn't understand, to board a troop train heading north. But at the border they were stopped. It was then that Elder Seibold pulled out the letter written by the military policeman in Cologne. And that letter, which he received only because of his own stubbornness, won him and his friends safe passage out of the country.

In all, Elder Seibold had collected seventeen of the thirty-one missing missionaries. The other fourteen had made it out on their own or through the help of Elder Kest. Of the 150 missionaries, every person made it out of the country to safety.

Rescued by Strangers

KEVIN STOKER

Elders David and Amasa Howard were going home.

From 1910–13, they had preached the restored gospel to the people of England. Now David was bound for the town of Nuneaton to meet his brother and enjoy a farewell party with local members and missionaries before sailing for America.

But their joyful reunion was short-lived, and their celebration never materialized. Instead, the brothers met just in time to discover the Church meetinghouse surrounded by nearly five hundred angry people itching for a fight.

The people were upset because a local family—a mother, her four daughters, and a son—had recently left town with a "Mormon elder" headed for Utah. Many in the mob were saying the missionary had taken the women back to Utah for immoral purposes.

Amasa had the misfortune of looking like the missionary who had helped the family immigrate, and David had the misfortune of being Amasa's brother. When the mob saw the brothers, they seized them and dragged them toward the river. Leaders of the crowd declared that they would drown the Mormons. The rioters beat Amasa and David with sticks and clubs every step of the way. Amasa was stabbed in the back with a knife but was not seriously injured.

Several policemen came to the brothers' rescue, but the mob was so large and unruly that even the lawmen backed off, leaving the pair to face the people's wrath alone.

The mob, kicking and shoving its helpless quarry, was nearing the river when three young men, whom no one recognized, tore into the crowd with such strength and force that the people retreated and let them through. The stout strangers opened a pathway through the angry mob, allowing Amasa and David to dash through a door and enter an archway fronting the street. They then climbed over a back fence and escaped down an alley.

"I shall always believe that those three young men were not just ordinary men, but were sent from our Heavenly Father for our deliverance," wrote David several years later. "They were able to hold back a mob still consisting of some three hundred fifty enraged people. Such strength is not given man, but is given by our Heavenly Father for the deliverance of His servants."

The Time Is Far Spent

ELIZA R. SNOW

The time is far spent; there is little remaining
To publish glad tidings by sea and by land.
Then hasten, ye heralds; go forward proclaiming:
Repent, for the kingdom of heaven's at hand.

Shrink not from your duty, however unpleasant,
But follow the Savior, your pattern and friend.
Our little afflictions, tho painful at present,
Ere long, with the righteous, in glory will end.

What, tho, if the favor of Ahman possessing,
This world's bitter hate you are called to endure?
The angels are waiting to crown you with blessings!
Go forward, be faithful, the promise is sure.

Be fixed in your purpose, for Satan will try you;
The weight of your calling he perfectly knows.
Your path may be thorny, but Jesus is nigh you;
His arm is sufficient, tho demons oppose.

$\mathcal{H}$e Commanded the Waves to Be Still

HENRY D. TAYLOR

The Lord has endowed some individuals with a gift and capacity for possessing and exercising great powers of faith. Such a man was Henry A. Dixon. Although married and with a family of many children, when called by the First Presidency to fill a mission to Great Britain, he readily accepted the call without hesitation. With three missionary traveling companions, he embarked from St. John Island at Newfoundland on the steamship *Arizona*.

En route a furious storm arose. As the missionaries were preparing to have their evening prayers prior to retiring, they felt a shocking jolt that caused the entire ship to quiver. As they rushed to the deck they discovered that the ship, traveling at full speed, had rammed a gigantic iceberg. A huge, gaping hole had been torn in the prow of the vessel, which extended even below the water line. The captain advised that only in a calm sea could he and the crew bring the ship to the nearest port, which was some 250 miles away.

The wind and the storm continued unabated. Many hours later and unable to sleep, Elder Dixon arose, dressed, and walked to the deck. Standing there alone in the dark, with deep humility and great faith, by the power of the Holy Priesthood, he rebuked the waves and commanded them to be still.

Thirty-six hours later the ship was able to return and dock at Port St. John. In accordance with Elder Dixon's promise, not a single life had been lost.

When the ship's owner, a Mr. Guion, learned of the accident, and knowing that Mormon missionaries were aboard, he was quoted as saying: "There is nothing to worry about. My line has transported Mormon missionaries for forty years and has never lost a boat with Mormon missionaries aboard!"

The Lord's Blessings

AMASA POTTER

In the Spring of 1856, in the days of my youth, I was called by the First Presidency of the Church of Jesus Christ of Latter-day Saints to go on a mission to Australia, to preach the gospel. I was young and inexperienced, and had but very little education. I had been to school but six months in my life, although I had been raised in the Church from infancy, and had been taught by my mother that God had spoken from the heavens in these last days and had sent a holy angel to reveal the gospel that had been lost from the earth. These things I understood; but the scriptures I never had read, from the fact that I could not read. Under these circumstances I went to President Heber C. Kimball and asked permission to stay at home one year, and I would go to school and learn to read and write, and then I would go. But he said that he had called me to a mission and he wanted me to go now. I received my endowments, and President Kimball blessed me and prophesied many great things which should happen to me in the next three years and a half; for he said that I would be gone that time, and should learn to read and write by my close application and the help of the Holy Spirit. I bade farewell to my aged mother and started, in company with some other Elders, for Australia. . . .

. . . In thirty-six days we arrived at Sydney, Australia, having sailed about 10,000 miles and had a pleasant voyage. . . .

We found the opposition to the gospel very great in this place, so I started, in company with another young Elder, to go to the interior of the island to commence our labors preaching the gospel. When we came to a city called Camden, forty miles from Sydney, we concluded to try to get a place to preach in. We were refused all public houses that we asked for. Finally we tried to get the privilege of stopping at a public house, or tavern, all night. We told the landlord that we were missionaries of the Church of Jesus Christ of Latter-day Saints, and we were traveling without purse or scrip, according to the pattern that Jesus had left on record in the Bible. The landlord asked us if we were "Mormons." We said that we were called that name by the world. After talking some time with him he ordered us out of the house, and told some drunken Irishmen to run us out of the town and he would give them a gallon of rum each. It was now after dark, and we went down one of the streets and called at a large boot and shoe shop. The owner said that he would keep us and we were having a good discussion on the principles of the gospel when a rough voice called to the master of the place, and said,

"Are you going to keep them d——d Mormons here all night?"

We looked towards the door and saw there a mob of drunken men, armed with native war clubs, spears and the boomerang. The boomerang is a weapon with which the natives formerly fought.

I said to my companion, "We must get out of here."

He replied, "How shall we do it without getting hurt?"

I told him that God had not sent us here to be killed in this manner, and if we would now trust wholly in the Lord, He would deliver us.

I had no more than said these words when the owner of the house caught the same spirit as the mob and said to us, "Get out of my house, or I will kill you," and, at the same time, struck at my partner with a hammer, but missed him as he sprang to one side.

The mob said, "Drive them out and we will use them up in a hurry."

I picked up my carpet-bag and umbrella and went to the door with a prayerful heart to God that he would protect us, and I walked out between many of them. It appeared that they did not see me or they did not notice me. The mob was arranged on both sides of the door, with their weapons drawn ready to strike at the first sight of us; and as my partner came out the leader of the band called the attention of his men to give some instructions how to deal with us, and thus he slipped past them unseen. I took him by the arm and we started down the street. In the darkness of the night they could not see us. About this time the owner of the house came to the door and they asked him where the "Mormons" were. He replied that they had gone out just that minute. They said they knew better; "for," said they, "they have not passed us, and you had better bring them out, or we will knock your house down." At that they broke into the house and, not finding us, they took the master and journeymen out and beat them almost to death.

In this deliverance we see the prediction of President Heber C. Kimball fulfilled; for he said that I should be brought into many close places, and it would seem that death stared me in the face; but, if I would be faithful to my mission, the angels of God would deliver me in all trials, and I should return in safety to the Church and to my home. In all of my travels on that island for two years and a half, I found that when there was a good work to be done in a city, we met with the greatest opposition; for in this same place, where we received such cruel treatment, we afterwards preached, and baptized, and organized a branch of the Church with many members.

Delivered from the Evil One

WILFORD WOODRUFF

On the 1st of July, 1838, one of the most interesting events transpired of my whole life in the ministry.

When Father Joseph Smith gave me my patriarchal blessing, among the many wonderful things of my life, he promised me that I should bring my father's household into the kingdom of God, and I felt that if I ever obtained the blessing, the time had come for me to perform it.

By the help of God, I preached the gospel faithfully to my father's household and to all that were with him, as well as to my other relatives, and I had appointed a meeting on Sunday, the 1st of July, at my father's home.

My father was believing my testimony, as were all in his household, but upon this occasion the devil was determined to hinder the fulfillment of the promise of the patriarch unto me.

It seemed as though Lucifer, the son of the morning, had gathered together the hosts of hell and exerted his powers upon us all. Distress overwhelmed the whole household, and all were tempted to reject the work. And it seemed as though the same power would devour me. I had to take to my bed for an hour before the time of meeting. I there prayed unto the Lord with my whole soul for deliverance, for I knew the power of the devil was exercised to hinder me from accomplishing what God had promised me.

The Lord heard my prayer and answered my petition, and when the hour of meeting had come I arose from my bed, and could sing and shout for joy to think I had been delivered from the power of the evil one.

Filled with the power of God, I stood up in the midst of the congregation and preached the gospel of Jesus Christ unto the people in great plainness.

At the close of the meeting we assembled on the banks of the Farmington river, "because there was much water there," and I led six of my friends into the river and baptized them for the remission of their sins.

All of my father's household were included in this number, according to the promise of the Patriarch. . . .

It was truly a day of joy to my soul. My father, stepmother and sister were among the number baptized. I afterwards added a number of relatives. I felt that this day's work alone amply repaid me for all my labor in the ministry.

Who can comprehend the joy, the glory, the happiness and consolation that an Elder of Israel feels in being an instrument in the hands of God of bringing his father, mother, sister, brother, or any of the posterity of Adam through the door that enters into life and salvation? No man can, unless he has experienced these things, and possesses the testimony of Jesus Christ and the inspiration of Almighty God.

$\mathcal{M}$y Pocket Bible

LORENZO SNOW

I spent the . . . winter [of 1838–39] in travel and preaching, chiefly in the northern part of Kentucky, with varied success, and treatment—sometimes received in the most courteous manner and listened to with intense interest, and, at other times, abusively and impudently insulted; but in no instance treated worse than was Jesus, whom I profess to follow. On [one] occasion, one evening, I was preaching in a large room of a private house, and afterwards learned that a portion of my audience had gathered for the purpose of mobbing me. They had arranged with a party that lay concealed at a little distance, and within call, to join them immediately on my leaving the house to return to my lodgings, and all proceed together to execute their schemes of vengeance. It was a very cold night, and after the close of the services I stood with my back to the chimney fire, with a number of others—some of whom belonged to the mob party. One of the latter persons, amid the jostling of the crowd, accidentally brought his hand in contact with one of the pockets in the skirt of my coat, which struck him with sudden alarm on his feeling, what he supposed to be, a large pistol. He immediately communicated the discovery to his affrighted coadjutors, all of whom directly withdrew, and, to their fellows outside, imparted the astounding news that the "Mormon" Elder was armed with deadly weapons. That was sufficient—the would-be outlaws abandoned their evil designs for fear of signal punishment; but the supposed pistol which caused their alarm and my protection, was my pocket Bible, a precious gift to me from the dearly beloved Patriarch, Father Joseph Smith.

"Wicked Men Can't Sing like Angels"

GEORGE ALBERT SMITH

Two humble missionaries, after walking until late in the afternoon in the sun in the heat of summer, came to a small house that was at the bottom of a hill. When the missionaries arrived, they found friends who invited them in to partake of their meager refreshment. And then they were asked to go outside in the cool of the afternoon shade, on one of those comfortable, open southern porches between two rooms, and sing some hymns. The people were not members of the Church, but they enjoyed Latter-day Saint hymns.

The missionaries had been threatened in that section. One of the men who had threatened them kept watch of the road and in that way learned when they arrived. He sent word to his associates, who saddled their horses and took their guns, and rode to the top of the hill overlooking the little house. The missionaries knew nothing about it; they did not know that right over their heads, not very far away, were a considerable number of armed horsemen. But they had the Spirit of the Lord, and as they sat there in the cool of the afternoon and sang hymns, the one hymn that seemed to have been prepared for the occasion was "Do What Is Right." They happened to be good singers, and their voices went out into the quiet air. They had only sung one verse when the leader of the mob took off his hat. They sang another verse, and he got off his horse, and the others got off their horses, and by the time the last verse had been sung, those men were repentant. Upon the advice of their leader, they rode away without making their presence known. The leader was so impressed with what he heard the missionaries sing that he said to his associates: "We made a mistake. These are not the kind of men we thought they were. Wicked men can't sing like angels, and these men sing like angels. They must be servants of the Lord."

The result was that this man became converted to the Church and later was baptized. And I never hear that hymn sung but I think of that very unusual experience when two missionaries, under the influence of the Spirit of God, turned the arms of the adversary away from them and brought repentance into the minds of those who had come to destroy them.

"Your God Is a God of Power"

KEVIN STOKER

On the night of May 5, 1852, Elder James S. Brown and his handful of Polynesian converts held a testimony meeting, then prayed. They didn't sleep, because outside the Mormons' meeting place, a mob of young braves were boasting of roasting the "fat missionary" while they danced and yelled through the night. Elder Brown had encountered fierce opposition since coming to Raivavae, a small island located more than four hundred miles south of Tahiti. Now the island leaders had decided during the night to burn the Mormon missionary.

On the afternoon of May 6, two large warriors armed with clubs burst into the hut and took Elder Brown to the beach. Most of the island's people had gathered there, with about thirty old councilors and fifteen stout warriors standing near a large, burning pile of wood and coral. In front of the boisterous crowd of islanders stood the missionary and his faithful converts. Stepping toward the mob, a convert named Rivae declared: "If you burn this man, you burn me first." His wife, holding her eight-month-old baby, rushed to his side and shouted, "I am a Mormon, and this baby is a Mormon, for 'nits make lice,' [a phrase used by the men who shot Mormon children at the Haun's Mill Massacre] and you will have to burn all of us, or Mormonism will grow again."

The leader of the opposition raced past the couple and confronted Elder Brown. Motioning to the now blistering bonfire, the chief bellowed: "Look, there is the fire. It is made to consume the flesh off your bones."

At that moment, Elder Brown, under the influence of the Spirit, proclaimed: "In the name of Israel's God, I defy ten of your best men, yea, the host of you, for I serve that God who delivered Daniel from the den of lions, and the three Hebrew children from the fiery furnace." As soon as he finished speaking, Elder Brown stood his ground before his accusers. The old councilors started verbally disputing with the young braves. Soon a fight broke out among them, and in the confusion that followed the Mormons slipped safely away.

Two months later, one of the old councilors ran away when he saw Elder Brown. The missionary chased the man down and asked him why he had fled. "Your God is a God of power, and I was afraid to meet His servant," the old native cried. Then he recalled the day the warriors had tried to burn the missionary. "At the moment that you defied us there was a brilliant light, or pillar of fire, [bearing] down close over your head. . . . We thought that you had prayed to your God of Power, and that he had sent the fire to burn us and our people if we harmed you. The young men did not see the light. They were going to burn you, and we tried to stop them. So we got into a fight."

Member Missionaries

"My Courage Was Put to a Test"

ANITA R. CANFIELD

Paul believed in victory, no matter how long and hard the road. I traveled some of [the Apostle] Paul's roads by automobile. He walked every mile. Those routes, roads, and distances covered by Paul are staggering. It must have been terribly difficult. It must have required tremendous sacrifice. He taught us by his hard work a great example of having courage, even when persecuted and oppressed.

I traveled with clients recently, and my courage was put to a test. Many of my clients have the luxury of traveling by private jet. Usually when we get on board, there is no socializing of any kind. We spread our plans or construction documents on a table and everyone talks about the project we are working on.

But this occasion was different. Their large plane was being serviced so we took a smaller, eight-passenger jet.

I found myself in the back of the plane; my clients, husband and wife, were seated in front of me. It was a small cabin and our knees almost touched as we faced each other. There was no way to pull out documents or discuss design details, and they seemed to want to just visit.

They asked about my family. They asked about my son on his mission. Then, out of nowhere the husband asked me, "How on earth did you get into this Mormon deal anyway?"

Normally I would take an opportunity like this to bear my testimony. But you need to know that this man can be extremely coarse and caustic at times. And he has teased me constantly about being "Mormon." He makes jokes about tithing and the time I spend at church or in Church service. . . .

The teasing perhaps is meant to be a sign of friendship, but sometimes it has been just plain ridiculous.

So at this moment I hesitated, unsure of how I should answer. Should I just give a generic response about my parents converting when I was a young child? It flashed through my mind that if I told him more I could open myself up to more teasing and caustic jabs.

Suddenly I thought of Paul and his hard work—and the intense persecution. And I thought of my missionary son, who was walking in Paul's footsteps as a missionary. Their sacrifices for the truth's sake pierced my heart, and I felt a powerful spirit envelop me.

I bore my testimony to them of how my parents had converted and how I had come to my own desire to know the truth about religion. I told them my conversion story and was able to tell them that I knew the Church was true and why. I stated that President Hinckley was the prophet and told them of my understanding of the Book of Mormon.

For twenty minutes I spoke with the power and sweetness that comes only by the Holy Ghost. I knew they felt something. They asked me to tell them of my husband's conversion story as well.

To this day, my client has not teased me anymore.

The Shoemaker Bears His Testimony

JOHN A. WIDTSOE

Soon after her arrival in Trondhjem, Anna Widtsoe rented an apartment for herself and her two boys in Steensbakken (Steens Hill) which was then being invaded by residences. . . .

In these two rooms she proceeded to make a home and to look the future in the face. . . . She was kept busy enough with household cares, dressmaking, and reading and studying her Bible. . . .

One day she asked a neighbor, a ship's captain living in the same house, an older resident, to recommend a shoemaker to whom she might take her son's shoes for repair. One Olaus Johnsen, a very competent, honest workman was recommended. In fact the shoemaker's son, Arnt, (at this writing living in Logan, Utah), brought to the house a pair of the captain's shoes, and took with him for repair, a pair of John's shoes. When the boy's shoes were returned, a Mormon tract was stuffed in each shoe. A little later with a parcel containing another pair of old shoes, the widow set forth in the warm sunshine of the spring of 1879 for the half-hour walk to Johnsen's shoemaker shop. It certainly did not occur to her that she was making the most fateful visit of her life. . . .

Olaus Johnsen was a wholesome, well-spoken man in his forties, a workman who knew his craft. His wife was of the sturdy Norwegian type. Anna Widtsoe first met the wife, and made inquiry about the meaning of the tracts found in her son's shoes that had been returned, repaired. Mrs. Johnsen declared that they told the truth, but that Mr. Johnsen would explain the whole matter.

The shoemaker agreed to put soles on the shoes strong enough to last a good while even under the wear of a lively, active lad, who was always moving about. . . . The widow was about to leave the shop, yet a little curious about the tracts which she had found in the first pair of shoes when they were returned, but unwilling to ask too many questions.

Anna Widtsoe's hand was on the door latch, when the shoemaker said, somewhat hesitatingly, for the business was concluded and the lady was a stranger, "You may be surprised to hear me say that I can give you something of more value than soles for your child's shoes." She was surprised. She looked into the eyes of the man, who stood straight and courageous in his shop.

"What can you, a shoemaker, give me better than soles for my son's shoes? You speak in riddles," she answered.

The shoemaker did not hesitate. "If you will but listen, I can teach you the Lord's true plan of salvation for His children. I can teach you how to find happiness in this life, and to prepare for eternal joy in the life to come. I can tell you whence you came, why you are upon the earth, and where you will go after death. I can teach you as you have never known it before, the love of God for His children on earth."

Understanding, happiness, joy, love—the words with which she was wrestling! But this was a shoemaker's shop. This man was clearly a humble man who knew little of the wisdom of schools and churches. She felt confused. She simply asked, "Who are you?" "I am a member of the Church of Christ—we are called Mormons. We have the truth of God." Mormons! It was terrible. She had innocently walked into a dangerous place. Hurriedly she thanked the shoemaker, left the shop, and climbed the hill.

Yet, as she walked homeward, the words of the shoemaker rang in her ears; and she remembered a certain power in his voice and majesty in his bearing when he delivered his message and bore his testimony. He was a shoemaker, but no ordinary man. Could it really be that the Mormons had the truth of the Lord? No, it was absurd! But, it made her thoughtful and restless. When the repaired shoes were brought to the house a day or two later, by the shoemaker's young son, Arnt Johnsen, Anna Widtsoe found, carefully tucked into each shoe, a Mormon tract. The shoemaker was valiant. He missed no opportunity to fulfill the obligation of a Latter-day Saint, to bear witness modestly and properly but steadily, to all the world.

Then began two years of struggle.

The tracts in the shoes aroused her curiosity, to the extent that one Sunday she went to a Mormon meeting. The meeting room was on the second floor of the shoemaker's home, a sturdy log house. A small group of people were there; and a fiery speaker, a missionary, raised all manner of questions in her mind. The main effect of that meeting was a resentment against the primitive environment of the meeting, and the quality of the people who constituted the membership of the Trondhjem branch. . . .

Soon, however, all was forgotten in her battles with the shoemaker and the missionaries upon points of doctrine. She knew her Bible. Time upon time she came prepared to vanquish the elders, only to meet defeat herself. She had not read the Bible as these men did. Gradually she began to comprehend that her reading had been colored and overshadowed by the teachings of the church of her childhood; and that these men, these Mormon missionaries, accepted the Bible in a truer, more literal manner. She liked it. Nevertheless she fought fearlessly. It was no use. At length she had to admit that the Bible was all on the side of the Mormons.

Even then she was not ready. There were other matters to be settled. Questions of authority, revelation, life within the Church, and a hundred others that her quick mind formulated, were presented to the missionaries, debated, discussed and taken up again. She had a worthy teacher in the missionary then in Trondhjem, Elder Anthon L. Skanchy, whose knowledge of the Gospel was extensive and sound, and whose wisdom in leading inquirers to truth was unusually fine. This well-informed, intelligent widow tested his powers. Upon her he directed the full battery of Gospel evidence. Unwillingly, yet prayerfully, she became convinced that she was in the presence of eternal truth.

At length, on April 1, 1881, a little more than two years after she first heard the Gospel, she was baptized into the Church by Elder Anthon L. Skanchy. Thin ice still lay over the edges of the fjord, which had to be broken to permit the ordinance to be performed. The water was icy cold. Yet, she declared to her dying day that never before in all her life she felt warmer or more comfortable than when she came out of the baptismal waters of old Trondhjem's fjord. The fire within was kindled, never to be extinguished. The humble people of the branch became her brethren and sisters. She loved them, and rejoiced in their company.

All this is easily told; but who can tell the full story of the spiritual and mental battles, the inner struggles, of those who must lay by the whole of their past lives, as it were, to accept the new-found truth? . . . Those who have charged that men and women accept Mormonism for ulterior motives know little of the intense search for truth and exhausting conquest of self that have preceded conversion. Only along the path of sacrifice does the Latter-day Saint enter into his joy. A gladness of soul it is, indeed, when the certainty of truth begins to glorify life. Peace is restored. The price seems small for so great a jewel. Anna Widtsoe found it so. Never, during her life did she speak of sacrifices for the Gospel, but always of the blessings that it had brought to her.

Brightly Beams Our Father's Mercy

PHILIP PAUL BLISS

Editor's Note: The metaphor of "lower lights" in this beloved hymn refers to the lights located at the base of many lighthouses. During storms, sailors align the light emanating from these lamps with that of the lighthouse above to navigate their craft through the channel and "make the harbor." Many a "struggling seaman" has been saved from the perils of the sea by the glow of the lower lights.

Brightly beams our Father's mercy
From his lighthouse evermore,
But to us he gives the keeping
Of the lights along the shore.

Dark the night of sin has settled;
Loud the angry billows roar.
Eager eyes are watching, longing,
For the lights along the shore.

Trim your feeble lamp, my brother;
Some poor sailor, tempest-tossed,
Trying now to make the harbor,
In the darkness may be lost.

Let the lower lights be burning;
Send a gleam across the wave.
Some poor fainting, struggling seaman
You may rescue, you may save.

"Saturday Is Fine"

ROBERT E. WELLS

A friend of mine lived next door to a nonmember neighbor for thirty years. The two families developed very close relationships. Over the years my friend's efforts produced interesting spiritual results. The neighbor's wife joined the Church. The neighbor's children joined the Church. The neighbor's sons went on missions. But for thirty years the father was not interested in changing his lifestyle nor his religious status.

My friend, in telling the story, laughed about his "almost" converted neighbor who would attend meetings from time to time. The neighbor always accompanied his family when a family member was taking part in a meeting, such as speaking in a missionary farewell or homecoming, giving a sermon in sacrament meeting, or performing a musical number. He also attended the LDS funerals of friends who passed away. This man even admitted that he thought that Mormon funerals were the best funerals he ever attended.

One day my friend visited the dental clinic of his long-time neighbor, who also happened to be the family dentist. Sitting in the dentist's chair waiting, my friend suddenly had a jolt of inspiration. When the dentist came in to attend him, my friend sat up, looked the dentist in the eye, and asked, "Doctor, would you please do me a great favor?" Innocently, the dentist answered readily, "Sure. What do you need?" My friend responded, "This is a big favor. Will you really do something very important for me?" The dentist knew his patient well and said, "Oh, come on. I've lent you my ladders, tools, and lawn mower. I've lent you my boat and my pickup. You know that anything I've got you can borrow." My friend, the patient, was serious. "Doctor," he said, "would you do me the biggest favor I can think of? Will you let me baptize you next Saturday?"

The dentist looked at his friend for a while without either of them saying a word. Then the dentist responded softly, "You've never put it quite that way before, Frank. I guess it's about time, isn't it? Yes, Saturday is fine!" My friend baptized his next-door neighbor after thirty years of going around an invisible wall!

Every Day She Would Go to the Market

SPENCER W. KIMBALL

Down in South America there was one woman who had joined the Church, and she loved it so much that every day she would go to the market place where lots of women came and there she'd say, "Have you ever heard of the Mormon boys?" The women would say, "No." "Well, you know, we have two that come and preach the gospel in our home. Why don't you come over and listen to them?" And do you know that that one middle-aged woman brought in ninety-one members of the Church? She would introduce them to the missionaries, and the missionaries taught them. Ninety-one!

$\mathcal{T}$he Only Phone on the Block

ROBERT E. WELLS

W e don't have a telephone in our home," [a friend of mine] told me. "There is a long waiting list to get a phone in our neighborhood [in Chile]. I have paid for one, but it will be another year or more before we get it. In the meantime, when we have an emergency, we go to the home of a friend on the other side of our block. It is the closest phone to us and the only one on our block. They are good people and very willing to let us use it, but we try to not bother them except for important Church matters or family emergencies.

"Each time one of us would ask to use their telephone we would take a new copy of the Church magazine, the *Liahona,* or a tract or new booklet for them to read. We have given them a family home evening manual and a copy of the Book of Mormon. We have asked if they would come to church with us or allow the missionaries to come to their home to talk about the Church, but they always showed no interest.

"One day, soon after we started praying for success and look-ing for daily opportunities to ask the golden questions, I received an emergency call via our neighbors' telephone. It was about the tragic death of a member, and I needed to help with some funeral arrangements. The family could hear my expressions of condo-lences and could ascertain what had happened.

"After I had finished my conversation, I thanked them for the use of their phone and apologized profusely for taking so much time. They showed interest in the tragedy, which I explained as briefly as I could. Noticing their tender concern, I asked, 'How much do you know about our church and our point of view about death and the certainty of resurrection, just like Christ was resurrected?' They admitted that they knew nothing about our doctrines or philosophies, so I asked, with a prayer in my heart, 'Would you like to know more about how we look upon the life after death in the spirit world and the resurrection?' They expressed interest so I invited them to my home. . . . They came, met the missionaries, listened, and in a few weeks the entire family was baptized."

He laughed after telling the story and advised me, "Now I am walking two blocks in the other direction to use another telephone just so I can give them a chance to let their phone do some Church work and maybe bring them into the Church the same way!"

The Governor's Copy of
the Book of Mormon

GEORGE ALBERT SMITH

During Word War I, I was in Washington, D.C., and wrote New York's Governor Charles Seaman Whitman telling him that on my way home I would like to stop and pay my respects to him. I received a telegram: "Come right along. I will receive you here."

But I found myself in Albany a day early. The Governor was out of town. I left the telephone number of my hotel with the Governor's secretary, and then contacted the missionaries. They were going to visit the home of one of the families of Saints that evening, and I was invited to go along. I left that telephone number with the hotel clerk.

About nine o'clock that evening the telephone rang. The sister answered it and reported, "Brother Smith, the Governor of New York wants to talk to you."

"You are certainly coming to see me, aren't you?" the voice on the telephone asked.

"I stopped here for that purpose," I said. "What time shall I come?"

"Ten o'clock."

"Ten o'clock tomorrow morning?"

"Ten o'clock tonight—at the Governor's mansion, not at the office."

I went back to the missionaries, saying that one of them would have to come and help me find the Governor's mansion. One of them offered to come, and we said good-bye to those Saints who had entertained us in their home.

The mansion was surrounded by guards as a wartime

precaution. We had a little difficulty convincing them that we had an appointment at that hour.

But finally [we] were past the gate and introduced to the Governor who said: "Come with me and we will go up to my den and we will have a good time together; no one will bother us up there."

Surrounded by the Governor's library, the three of us talked. Finally, the conversation turned to the war, and the Governor was happily surprised at the number of L. D. S. boys that I told him were in the services. And of how we had supported the bond drives.

"You have done better than we have done. But, how is this war coming out?"

"Don't you know, Governor?" I asked.

"No, I don't know who is going to win it."

"Well," I said, "where is your Book of Mormon?"

He turned around in his swivel chair and reached into the book cupboard behind him, and laid a copy of the Book of Mormon on the table in front of me. And the young missionary's eyes fairly popped out of his head. Here we were in the home of the Governor of the State of New York and he had a Book of Mormon.

"Governor," I said, "I am not going to take a lot of time, but you can find out right in here how this war is coming out. We are going to win the war." I read to him what is found in the Book of Mormon with reference to this people and this nation, in which the Lord told us: "There shall be no kings upon this land which shall rise up unto the Gentiles . . . I, the Lord, the God of heaven, will be their king," and then he refers to the fact that if we keep his commandments we have the promise from him of his preservation and his watchcare.

"I had not seen that," the Governor said.

I replied: "You are not doing a very good job reading your Book of Mormon."

I laid the book down, and our visit continued. Out of the corner of my eye I saw the young missionary pick up that book. I knew what he was wondering, just how the Governor had a copy. The missionary turned to the first page, and there he read the inscription: "To the Honorable Charles Seaman Whitman, Governor of New York, with compliments and best wishes of George Albert Smith."

The Best Years

ANITA R. CANFIELD

A husband and wife I'll call Jim and Martha brought hope back into their lives as they brought hope to someone else through love and service. They had been married thirty years. Their children were doing well, their financial security was established, they were enjoying life and each other, they were the best of friends. Then the devastating news came that Martha was dying. It was a slow-growing disease but an incurable one. She could expect to live two, maybe three more years. After the anger, denial, and sorrow of it all passed, they began to make plans. They would travel and visit their children and spend all their time together.

Then at a Church auxiliary meeting it came to Martha's attention that a family in their ward was in need. The husband was not active in the Church; the wife, who was not a member, had recently had a stroke and was paralyzed permanently. She was only twenty-nine years old and the couple had three small children. Their meager savings were gone, spent on hospital bills. The husband was struggling to look after the children, maintain a job, and care for his invalid wife.

Martha went home from that meeting touched deeply by the plight of these people. For the first time since hearing of her own condition, she felt the relief of being concerned for someone else. Through a sleepless night she thought about how good her life with Jim had been, how blessed and full. This illness was a mountain for them, but they had the hope of eternal life together someday. She knew they had the resources to alleviate some suffering for this young couple. What would the Savior do? For the first time in months she felt a brightness of hope. "This is right," she thought. She felt the Spirit moving her towards a love of God and of all men.

When morning came she told Jim of her restless night, of her promptings to help, of the hope she was feeling. She said that to travel would be nice, but after she was gone Jim would only have photographs and a few memories of that time. If they helped this family, Jim would see the fruits of their labors for years to come. She asked him if that wasn't what the gospel was all about? She could die having been productive to the end, and she said it would bring peace to everyone.

Jim could not disagree. He felt the Spirit, and he sensed renewed hope. That morning they knelt in prayer for guidance, for inspiration, for love. That evening they paid their first visit to this needy little family.

In the two years and eight months that followed they brought hope into the lives of this couple. They remodeled their living room, adding a bigger window so the mother could watch her children at play and be able to enjoy the outside. Jim and Martha bought her a special bed so she could be more comfortable by her window to the world. They worked hard planting a rose garden right in front of this window, and they also maintained the yard work. They spent countless hours tending the children and holding them, trying to comfort them as their mother no longer could. They took the children on short trips with them, to the park, on numerous picnics. They made sure they went to church every Sunday. Jim and Martha made special meals twice a week and had family home evening Monday with the family. It wasn't long before the father was attending church again. And soon after that his wife wanted the missionary lessons.

The stake missionaries were called in, and Jim and Martha helped make every meeting a special event. It was a joyous and emotional day when Jim helped lower this young wife and mother into the baptismal font. Tears streamed down his cheeks as he helped support her fragile body while her husband raised his hand to the square and began, "Having been commissioned of Jesus Christ . . ."

That night Martha told Jim, "These have been the best years of my life. I love the Lord, I love life, I am at peace."

Martha was too ill to attend the temple to see them sealed. But Jim reported back every detail, and when the photographs arrived she lovingly memorized each one. Martha passed away several months later.

The fast Sunday after the funeral, the young husband bore his testimony of the Savior's love in his life. He said he had seen the Savior on the faces of Jim and Martha. Love, he said, had brought back hope into his life and the lives of his family. Even the hope, he wept, of eternal life.

Not long after that his wife also died. . . .

A love of God and of all men brings a true and perfect brightness of hope, even to the end.

Reactivation

A Plea for Those Who Err

HENRY A. TUCKETT

Think gently of the erring one;
    O let us not forget,
However darkly stained by sin,
    He is our brother yet.

Heir of the same inheritance,
    Child of the selfsame God,
He hath but stumbled in the path
    We have in weakness trod.

Speak gently to the erring ones;
    We yet may lead them back,
With holy words, and tones of love,
    From misery's thorny track.

Forget not, brother, thou hast sinned,
    And sinful yet mayst be;
Deal gently with the erring heart,
    As God has dealt with thee.

"We Are Here to Welcome
You into the Ward"

ANITA R. CANFIELD

Members of the Church around the world remember President Spencer W. Kimball's motto, Do It. That expression was a household phrase while he was our prophet. We had hope in those words because his example in "doing" made it believable. A few years before he died I was told the following story by the Relief Society president of the stake where President Kimball lived in Salt Lake City:

"It seems that a young man moved into one of the basement apartments with his girlfriend. This was at a time when this liberal behavior was just beginning to shake the roots of conservative Salt Lake City. This young man was the son of a prominent Church member. The ward was appalled and shocked at his arrogant behavior. Evidently the gossip and disapproval were running profusely.

"Then one Sunday he appeared at church. He returned again and again. Soon the girlfriend moved out. As time passed he participated in all the ordinances of the gospel. The reason for his change of heart was soon discovered.

"One Sunday afternoon he said he was watching football on television. His girlfriend was taking a nap. The doorbell rang, and he got up to open it. There standing on his porch were President and Sister Kimball with a loaf of homemade bread. The prophet extended his hand in friendship and said, 'Hello, I am Brother Kimball. This is my wife, Sister Kimball, and we are here to welcome you into the ward.'

"This young man was touched and shaken by the love of President and Sister Kimball. It was irresistible to him that one so

great would reach out in care and concern for him. It changed his
life."

$\mathcal{T}$he Prodigal Cowboy

ROBERT E. WELLS

$\mathbf{F}$ollowing my normal custom, I had asked the stake president of a stake in the western United States if there was anything I could do during my coming visit to his stake to encourage some of his prospective elders to return to activity.

The stake president phoned back to clear the schedule with me and said that if I could arrive early enough Saturday morning, he would set up a few interviews at his office in the stake center. He asked whether I wanted the wives to come in with their husbands. I told him that I preferred to have them come in alone because I was really going to lean on the brethren who were to be interviewed. He asked what I meant by that. So I explained my philosophy, which I had learned from General Authorities I had traveled with, especially the technique employed by Elder Delbert L. Stapley. . . .

One of the men who came in for an interview was a tall, lanky, fiftyish, prosperous rancher. The stake president told me some interesting background information about this good man (whom we'll call Joe). He was from a faithful LDS family and his parents were very active and had always been Church leaders. He had sent his sons on missions. His wife was a convert and active, but, according to the stake president, Joe was looked upon as being difficult to work with, uncooperative about church activity, and really quite rebellious for many years. The stake president said he was a prodigal whom they had tried for years to bring back.

Joe came to the interview straight from the corral, wearing his Levi's and his boots with still a little manure on the instep. In his western shirt pocket was a pack of cigarettes. Obviously he was not about to be impressed with a General Authority or anyone else, nor did he care to impress us.

I shook hands with him and invited him to sit down. I placed the stake president and the bishop on either side of Joe so that I faced all three of them. Following the indications of the Spirit, I first addressed the stake president and asked, trying to keep it light, "Is Joe a good man?" He acknowledged that yes, he was. I then asked the bishop the same unrehearsed question. "Yes," he allowed, "Joe is a good husband, a good father, and a good man."

"Joe," I asked, "are you as good a man as they think you are?" I was smiling and he smiled back a bit wanly, and said, "No. I think they are just trying to impress you."

My attempt at humor hadn't helped much, but I forged ahead. "Joe, I think you're a lot better than you'll admit to being, but these leaders love you and I love you. In this spirit of love can I ask you a few questions—three to start with?" He said, "Sure, go ahead."

My first question was, "Do you love your Heavenly Father?" He said that he did. The second question was, "Do you love the Savior and His church—this church?" From what I had been told, I was expecting him to give me trouble on this one, but I was pleasantly surprised. He said that he loved the Savior and the Church. The third question was, "Do you love your wife and are you faithful to her?" The answer was emphatically in the affirmative. "She is a lot better person than I am," he added.

Joe's answers and the spirit I felt from him convinced me that I could invite him to receive the greatest blessings that we, as judges in Israel could offer a man—to be ordained an elder and to be given a temple recommend. So I said to him, "What you have told me can qualify you to be ordained an elder and to be given a temple recommend in a few weeks, provided you comply with certain requirements. Who would be happiest to see you ordained and in the temple?"

Joe gulped in surprise, then slowly answered, "My wife, my kids, and my parents." Gratified with the way things were going, I continued, "I can see you must have a very supportive family, so now let's talk about the worthiness the Lord expects. Just three questions."

I reminded Joe that we were discussing some of the greatest blessings of this life and asked, "Will you attend all of your meetings from now on?" He responded in the same level tone of seriousness and with the same rhythm that I was using, but he was not making fun of me. "Yes, I will." I felt that he had just taken a major step in the right direction. I was praying for him to do just that, all the while loving this man sitting in front of me. However, I couldn't tell what was going through the minds of the stake president and the bishop.

"Second, will you observe the Word of Wisdom from now on?" He paused just an instant, and I thought he glanced down at his shirt pocket, but his gaze met mine and he said firmly, "Yes, I will." Then I asked, "Third, will you pay a full tithing from now on?" His answer indicated something else I had not been told. "Elder," he said, "I always pay a full tithing." The bishop and the stake president nodded affirmatively.

Just then a commotion was heard outside in the hall—some excited voices, followed by a knock at the door; without waiting, a man burst into the room. He apologized and explained there was an emergency for the president and the bishop. Already on their feet, the two brethren left. Joe strode over to the door, closed it, and locked it. He stood facing me with his hand behind him on the doorknob.

"Elder Wells," he said, "you probably think that you have just committed me to becoming active, don't you?" I nodded and admitted, "I didn't expect it to be a secret." "No, you don't understand, Elder. You didn't commit *me*, you committed *them!*"

"What do you mean by that?" I asked. "There must be something going on here that I really don't understand."

Still holding the doorknob, he said to me, "The bishop, the stake president, and I went to school together. We are the same age and were in the same class all the way. We were in Primary, Sunday School, and in the deacons, teachers, and priests quorums together. I was a bishop's son, and everyone expected me to be 'goody-goody' and to go on a mission. I guess I rebelled and didn't want to be told what I had to do, so I picked up some bad habits and married out of the Church, while the bishop and the stake president went on missions and married in the temple.

"Eventually my wife, who is really a special lady, joined the Church. Together we sent our kids on missions. Over the years my leaders have tried to reactivate me. In the interviews they have given me the impression that if I would become 'active,' someday—maybe someday—I might be good enough to be ordained an elder. And someday, way out there in the future, I might become good enough to go to the temple. . . .

". . . But you made me a different kind of deal. You didn't ask me to repent. You offered to ordain me and give me a temple recommend in a few weeks."

At this point I just had to interrupt him. "Joe, you understand that we are not talking about just a short time. We are talking about your being obedient forever." He nodded and said, "I know enough to understand exactly what you expect of me, but you said a few weeks and I can do that. I can do everything else from now on—and forever. But you committed them to believe in me."

The next day, dressed in a suit, this good brother attended conference with his family. They all looked like a glow of glory was over them. The entire row was occupied by their relatives. Before three months had passed, Joe was ordained an elder, and on schedule they were sealed in the temple. The stake president reported to me that they were happy to correct the erroneous impressions held by their boyhood companion and that the father and mother of this new elder, who were still alive, were present at the temple sealing, together with his leaders.

$\mathcal{A}$ Delinquent Elder

EZRA TAFT BENSON

At a stake presidency's meeting in Boise, Idaho, years ago, we were trying to select a president for the weakest and smallest elders quorum in the stake. Our clerk had brought a list of all the elders of that quorum, and on the list was the name of a man whom I had known for some years. He came from a strong Latter-day Saint family, but he wasn't doing much in the Church. If the bishop made a call to do some work on the chapel, he'd usually respond, and if the elders wanted to play softball, you would sometimes find him out playing with them. He did have leadership ability; he was president of one of the service clubs and was doing a fine job.

I said to the stake president, "Would you authorize me to go out and meet this man and challenge him to square his life with the standards of the Church and take the leadership of his quorum? I know there is some hazard in it, but he has the ability."

The stake president said, "You go ahead, and the Lord bless you."

After Sunday School I went to this man's home. I'll never forget the look on his face as he opened the door and saw a member of his stake presidency standing there. He hesitantly invited me in; his wife was preparing dinner, and I could smell the aroma of coffee coming from the kitchen. I asked him to have his wife join us, and when we were seated, I told him why I had come. "I'm not going to ask you for your answer today," I told him. "All I want you to do is to promise me that you will think about it, pray about it, think about it in terms of what it will mean to your family, and then I'll be back to see you next week. If you decide not to accept, we'll go on loving you," I added.

The next Sunday, as soon as he opened the door I saw there had been a change. He was glad to see me, and he quickly invited me in and called to his wife to join us. He said, "Brother Benson, we have done as you said. We've thought about it and we've prayed about it, and we've decided to accept the call. If you brethren have that much confidence in me, I'm willing to square my life with the standards of the Church, a thing I should have done long ago." He also said, "I haven't had any coffee since you were here last week, and I'm not going to have any more."

He was set apart as elders quorum president, and attendance in his quorum began going up—and it kept going up. He went out, put his arm around the inactive elders, and brought them in. A few months later I moved from the stake.

Years passed, and one day on Temple Square in Salt Lake City, a man came up to me, extended his hand, and said, "Brother Benson, you don't remember me, do you?"

"Yes, I do," I said, "but I don't remember your name."

He said, "Do you remember coming to the home of a delinquent elder in Boise seven years ago?" And then, of course, it all came back to me. Then he said, "Brother Benson, I'll never live long enough to thank you for coming to my home that Sunday afternoon. I am now a bishop. I used to think I was happy, but I didn't know what real happiness was."

Spiritual Rehabilitation

LUCILE C. TATE

Bishop [LeGrand] Richards sat in his office going over the priesthood rolls with his counselors. Like him, Elliott C. Taylor was a newcomer to the ward. Alexander R. Curtis had lived all his life in Sugar House, so it was mainly to him that the questions were directed.

"What about Brother A_____?" the bishop would ask.

"Oh, he's inactive. You can't get him to do anything," would be the answer.

Night after consecutive night they continued to review the alphabetical list, the bishop putting a check mark against all the "can't gets." When they had completed the survey, the bishop said: "Brethren, let's ask the stake president not to send us any home missionaries for a few months (only high councilors to check up on us), and let's ask each of these inactive men to speak in our sacrament meetings. By giving them twelve minutes apiece, we can have four speak every Sunday but fast day."

They visited each man on the list, became acquainted with his family, and invited him to speak, not upon a gospel subject but about what the Church meant to him, his family, and his pioneer ancestors. If the brother said he preferred not to give a talk, the bishop would smile and say, "Well, it's up to you, but on [giving a date about two weeks hence] we will announce you, and if are you not there we will tell the people that we came to your house and personally invited you, so they will know we didn't overlook you."

Almost to a man the inactive brethren responded, and with tears flooding their eyes and voices they would tell at the pulpit that in the twenty or thirty years since their mission reports, this was the first time they had been asked to speak in sacrament meeting. This experience taught Bishop Richards that "you can rehabilitate a man better spiritually by putting him at the pulpit than in any other way."

$\mathcal{B}$rother Clay

ANITA R. CANFIELD

$\mathbf{M}$y daughter Ashley served her mission in the Hawaiian Islands. . . . Halfway through her mission she was assigned to . . . the smaller island of Kauai. She and her companion were located in a small and somewhat remote area on this island.

The little branch they worked with was tucked away in this breathtakingly beautiful little corner of the islands. The time there was difficult because there was almost no one to teach. She felt discouragement because the work was so slow, so meager. She and her companion decided that they would create work. They decided to focus on the less-active families in the branch.

They made personal visits to these families and went around with a plan. When the door opened, here stood two lovely, radiant young women who introduced themselves as sister missionaries. Then they explained they had no one to teach the gospel to and were afraid they would forget their discussions, could they practice on this family? . . .

A "marvelous work and a wonder" took place the seven months she was there. Many came back.

Week after week she wrote of one particular family that I will call the Clays. Week after week we saw her love and hope grow for them. Week after week we looked forward to her report of their progress.

The Clays had been less active for many, many years. They had been married and divorced from each other three times. They were currently living together, but not married. They had three little girls.

Their lives had been filled with drug abuse and addiction,

alcoholism, and other serious spiritual problems. They were struggling physically, emotionally, and spiritually.

As Ashley and her companion came to bring the gospel back into their home, it was the wife who responded first. She had not been to church since she was thirteen or fourteen. The husband had not participated since he had been a teenager as well.

At the first meeting in their home, Brother Clay acknowledged the sister missionaries with a somewhat cool greeting, and then he left the room. Sister Clay listened to their discussion and responded positively enough to invite them to return. At the second visit she informed them he wasn't interested, he didn't want anything to do with the Church at all. That would be fine with them, Ashley told her, she was glad to be able to "practice" at least with Sister Clay.

Week after week they faithfully returned. Week after week they saw small changes taking place in Sister Clay. Her faith was rekindled, the flicker of a testimony began to be fanned back into a flame. She began to come to sacrament meeting. She began to bring her girls. She looked forward to the meetings with the sister missionaries. She spoke of her desires to return to the gospel. She began to be filled with real intent.

One visit became a turning point for Brother Clay. Ashley had the opportunity to ask him if he would join them. He was extremely negative and told her that the Church had been pushed at him too hard and that it had been more important to others than he was. He wanted nothing to do with it or the priesthood. At that opportunity she told him what the priesthood had meant to her.

. . . She told him how much it had meant to her to have a father who was worthy so that she could call upon him anytime for blessings of comfort and peace and courage. She expressed her feelings of gratitude and love for her father and how much his guidance and priesthood leadership had meant to her. She concluded by telling him she wondered where she would be now without it, probably not in Hawaii or on a mission. He had three daughters; she testified of the blessing the priesthood could be to them.

She watched the stiff defensiveness in his physical posture begin to relax. His face began to reveal that he was pondering her words. She felt a quiet spirit about him. She knew he was considering his own three young and adorable daughters. This time he listened to their discussion.

The next Sunday he came to church, and the Sunday after that, and kept coming Sunday after Sunday. At first they only stayed for sacrament meeting. He came in Aloha shirts and jeans and thongs.

One day a letter came from Ashley filled with excitement and joy. She was writing the day after fast and testimony meeting. Guess who, she wrote, had stood that morning and borne his testimony? Brother Clay! He had come to church in a new suit, white shirt, tie, and shoes. He had gone to the pulpit and borne his testimony that he knew the Church is true and wanted to come back fully. Then she wrote of a specific sentence he had said about her. Then she wrote: "Oh by the way, Mom, his mother knows you. You stayed in their home when you spoke in their stake. It was the stake where (and she cited a familiar name) was the stake president."

This startled me. I began to remember that visit nearly six years earlier. If Ashley had not named the stake president, I would never have been able to recall this experience with Brother Clay's parents. I remembered those parents, even the room I stayed in. The memories came flooding back.

During that talk I had shared hope and feelings of love for my own wayward, lost son. I spoke that day of hope and prayer and of a God who does hear and answer our prayers.

Brother Clay's parents drove me back to the airport after the conference. During that ride, they poured out their hearts to me of their love and hope for a son who had been gone from them and from the Church for many years. They had not even seen him in a long time. He was living in some remote village in the Hawaiian Islands.

They spoke of serious and sorrowful experiences with drugs and alcohol and the law. I didn't remember the details but I did remember their sorrow and I remembered the gravity of their son's situation. They even had a grandchild they had never seen. There seemed to be no hope, even after years of praying.

I remembered what happened next. There was a wonderful spirit in the car as we spoke and shared thoughts. Then suddenly, without forethought, I found myself saying and promising to them that one day there would come into their son's life someone who would touch his heart, and he would change!

I remember wondering later where that had come from. I had hoped it was the Spirit, I worried I had said the wrong thing. . . .

Who would have ever known six years before when I told this to his parents it would be my daughter? . . . I believe the Lord allowed Ashley and me to be a part of this witness that he is in charge. He knows his flock, the ones who have strayed and the ones who pray for them. His "hand is stretched out still."

"Can You Be Worthy for Ten Minutes?"

MARVIN J. ASHTON

Shortly before Christmas one year, I had the opportunity of going to the hospital at the request of a mother whose fifty-five-year-old son was seriously ill. As I met with them and tried to give them comfort, the patient's nephew was in the hospital room as well. The afflicted one's wife said, "Elder Ashton, would it be possible for you to give my husband a blessing?" I said yes. Then I looked in the direction of the thirty-year-old nephew and said, "Are you an elder?" He said, "Yes, I am an elder, but don't ask me to put my hands on his head. I am not worthy to participate in a blessing with you." As he backed away, I said, "Randy, how would you like to try to be worthy for ten minutes? Couldn't you be worthy for that long while you help me give this needed blessing?" He nodded his head and said, "I think I can be worthy for a few minutes." While he was coming over to the side of the bed I said, "If you can do it for ten minutes, you can do it for thirty minutes." He said, "Yes." I said, "If you can do it for thirty minutes, you can do it for a day, can't you?"

About then I felt he figured we had better get on with the blessing or he would be committed. We gave his uncle a blessing and when it was over he said, "Thank you for letting me share this blessing with you. No one has ever put it up to me like this before. I will try to be worthy."

Perhaps the best way to help some of our associates who are not quite as active as they should be is to involve them. I don't know of anything that would be more important and have more impact upon an inactive person than to have us call and say,

"Would you help me to administer to my wife, my roommate, or my friend?" We need to give them an opportunity to make shaping up a process.

Other Sheep I Have

WILLIAM CULLEN BRYANT

Look from the sphere of endless day,
Oh, God of mercy and of night!
In pity look on those who stray,
Benighted, in this land of light.

In peopled vale, in lonely glen,
In crowded mart by stream or sea,
How many of the sons of men
Hear not the message sent from thee.

Send forth thy heralds, Lord, to call
The thoughtless young, the hardened old,
A wandering flock, and bring them all
To the Good Shepherd's peaceful fold.

Send them thy mighty word to speak
Till faith shall dawn and doubt depart,
To awe the bold, to stay the weak,
And bind and heal the broken heart.

Then all these wastes, a dreary scene,
On which, with sorrowing eyes, we gaze,
Shall grow with living waters green,
And lift to heaven the voice of praise.

"Do You Know That Feeling?"

ANITA R. CANFIELD

When the president of a huge southern California stake Relief Society picked me up at the airport, she cautioned me to be prepared for a very poor turnout that night. She related all the troubles their stake had been experiencing. There had been unusual growth, wards had been divided, people were feeling left out—in one ward members were suing each other and there had been many excommunications. I felt like turning back right then!

She was right. Very few women showed up. I knew the attendance indicated that it was going to be a long hour at the pulpit. It was.

For a little over an hour I struggled for the Spirit. The congregation was not with me. The feeling in the room was flat. Apathy was so thick I could taste it. I wanted my talk to be over.

Then something changed during the last twenty minutes. I felt the women's hearts open up to the words and *feelings* of the message. We were together; we were one. The sweetest spirit filled the room.

During the closing song I heard my "mind" say, "Get up and tell them what it was." I thought, "No, this is the closing song. Thank goodness." Again, my "mind" said, "Get up, and tell them what it was." This time I argued, "No! Here comes the sister to give the closing prayer." Then, a third time, a very firm but very still and small voice came again, "Get up now!"

I scared the poor woman when I jumped up just as she stepped up to the pulpit to pray. "Excuse me," I said. "Do you know that feeling we all felt these last twenty minutes? Well, that is the Holy Ghost."

That was all. I sat down and never thought another thought about it until a year later when a letter arrived from a woman who had been in attendance that night. She wrote:

"I had been inactive for two years. I had asked my bishop to please excommunicate me. My friend asked me to please attend one last meeting before I went through with this severe step. It seemed harmless enough, and she had been a great support.

"The reason I sought excommunication was that, growing up in the Church, I had heard most of the members speak of the Holy Ghost as someone real to them. He was not real to me. I believed if I had never felt the Spirit I could not know the Church was true and should not be a member.

"When you stood up and said what you did about the Holy Ghost, my heart pounded! I had felt the change in the room the last part of the meeting. When you said it was the Holy Ghost, I knew it was! But something else important, I realized I had felt that same feeling *many* times all my life and just didn't know what it was!"

Example

"Who Taught You the Gospel?"

HAROLD B. LEE

There was an incident up in the post office in Salt Lake City, a little drama a few months ago. Two men had stood side by side sorting letters over the last twenty years, one a member of the Church and the other not. A few months ago, the nonmember turned to our Latter-day Saint and said, "Well, I'm going to be baptized into the Church next Saturday."

"You are?" said the Latter-day Saint. "Who taught you the gospel?"

"You did," said the man.

"I? Why, to my knowledge I've never discussed any of the principles of the Church with you."

"No," he said, "you're right. But twenty years now I've been standing by your side. I've sat with you at lunchtime. I've been out with you at outings. I've been in your home. I've been in your church. All that time I've never heard you tell a filthy or an obscene story. I've never heard you find fault or criticize. I find you to be loyal to your family, devoted to your church, a kind father and husband. This set me thinking, 'I'd like to belong to that man's church.' I began secretly to investigate the teachings of a church that produces a man like you. Because of you, I'm now ready to belong to that church; I want to be baptized."

"*I* Can't Figure You Out"

KEVIN STOKER

The new marine, Harlow Cheney, was tall and athletically built, but that wasn't what made him stand out from the other men in his platoon in 1944.

He was reserved, calm, and self-disciplined. He spent a lot of time meditating and reading the scriptures. The other marines indulged in drinking and partying, but Harlow rejected offers to join them. He didn't drink or smoke. Harlow's behavior puzzled Clifford Chebahtah, a burly Indian sergeant from the state of Oklahoma. One day while Harlow sat alone whittling on a stick, he was approached by the sergeant. "Cheney, I can't figure you out," Clifford said. "You don't do any of the things the other men do. You're all by yourself. You're just different. Where do you come from and why do you act this way?"

Harlow related that he was from Idaho and didn't do a lot of those things because his religion taught against it.

"Idaho," replied Clifford. "Don't tell me you're one of those Utah and Idaho Mormons!"

"Yep," Harlow said.

Clifford continued to watch the young Idahoan. He often asked Harlow about Mormonism. After some discussion, the Idahoan offered his sergeant a copy of the Book of Mormon, saying, "You ought to read this; it's about your ancestors."

Clifford turned down the Book of Mormon. He began wondering if this deeply religious soldier would be able to fire his rifle to kill another human being. In the heat of the battle, could he depend on the Mormon marine? Their company was headed for Japan's heavily fortified Pacific atoll of Iwo Jima. It was to be one of the bloodiest battles of World War II. Clifford voiced his fears to the unassuming Idahoan. Harlow told the sergeant he didn't need to worry. "I'll be with you, and I'll do all that is expected of me."

The night before the landing at Iwo Jima, Clifford retired deep into the ship to a place where he was sure he could be alone. He laid his weapons of war aside, then knelt down and prayed. He said that if the Lord spared his life, he would serve Him in any way he could. When Clifford's men hit the beach the next morning at Iwo Jima, they suffered heavy losses. After a few hours, most of the marines in Clifford's unit lay dead. Only five, including Harlow, had survived the initial battle, and all of them were wounded. They were evacuated to different hospitals, and Clifford would never see Harlow again.

Clifford returned to the United States, married, and settled in Anadarko, Oklahoma. He forgot about Harlow Cheney. In fact, he recalled his first name as Ralph, not Harlow Cheney. Then one night after he came home from work his wife told him to get dressed up because they were going to have company. Two LDS missionaries visited and taught his family the gospel. After he listened to their first discussion, he didn't want them to leave. He pleaded for them to stay "and tell me more." His family was baptized on July 3, 1949, along with thirty-five other people at a service attended by Elder Spencer W. Kimball, then an Apostle.

During the years before his death in January 1986, he longed to find Harlow Cheney and thank him for his example. But all efforts to find the missionary marine failed. However, when Delos and Verla Lusk returned to Sugar City, Idaho, from a mission to Oklahoma, they resumed the search for "Ralph" Cheney. They had about given up—especially after Clifford's death—but something kept them looking. Finally, while visiting with friends from Paul, Idaho, they looked at an alphabetical listing of the 27th Marine Battalion Replacement and found Harlow Cheney's name listed two lines below Clifford Chebahtah. Their friends were shocked. They knew a Harlow Cheney who lived only fifteen miles away in Heyburn, Idaho. The Lusks called Harlow and set up an appointment to meet him.

The first thing the Lusks asked him was if he remembered Clifford Chebahtah. He did. They then told him that Clifford and his family had joined the Church. It may have taken a few years, but the old sergeant had figured out why Harlow had been different.

Your Own Version

PAUL GILBERT

You are writing a Gospel,
    A chapter each day,
By deeds that you do,
    By words that you say.

Men read what you write,
    Whether faithless or true;
Say, what is the Gospel
    According to you?

The Fifth Time through
I Saw Christ's Mission

PAULL HOBOM SHIN

I was born in Korea, and when the Korean Conflict began in 1950, I fled south to escape the communist invasion. There I met the American military and obtained a position to work as a houseboy, which I continued for the next three years. Because I was a displaced person, I spent most of my childhood fending for myself. During that time I thought a lot about the pain of life. I was keenly interested in and constantly searched for a meaning to my life that would transcend the suffering and make it all worthwhile.

When I first met the American soldiers who were sacrificing their lives to help Korea, I felt that surely I could learn from them how to find happiness and peace. Very soon I became discouraged because of their conduct. Their heavy drinking, smoking, profanity, and generally unloving attitude toward Koreans did not seem to bring them happiness, and it certainly did not uplift me. One soldier, however, stood out from among the rest. He was different. He did not smoke, drink, or profane. In addition, he was friendly toward everyone. He even displayed a warm and loving disposition toward Koreans, often calling them brothers and sisters. I was so impressed with his life and example that I decided I wanted to become like him.

One day, I asked him why he was so different from the other soldiers, and he told me that he was a Mormon. Naturally I did not know anything about Mormonism, so I asked him to teach me. He gave me some preliminary background on the Church and then offered me a Book of Mormon. Now I am sure he did not fully realize the limits of my language ability—or education for that matter—when he asked me to read this book. Despite the fact that I could not read English, I admired Dr. Paull so much I determined to read the book at all costs. I took a quick ABC lesson from a fellow Korean, purchased an English-Korean dictionary, and started to read. I would read one word in the Book of Mormon, then I would refer to the dictionary for the meaning. I would write each word and its meaning down in a notebook. When I finished one sentence, I would try to translate the meaning with my own comprehension. At that time, we were not allowed light in the combat zone, so each night, even in the sweltering heat of the Korean summer, I would cover myself with a blanket to block out the light and read the Book of Mormon with a flashlight. It took me seven months to read the book once completely through.

When I finished that first time, I did not really understand what I had read. Mostly I had only connected with the continual war stories. I asked Dr. Paull how he had found the meaning of life in a book of unending war stories. He replied that perhaps I had missed the real point of the book and had better read it again! Because I could feel its importance to him, and I wanted to be like Dr. Paull, during the next three years I read the book five times, trying to penetrate its depth with my limited language and life experience. Each time I read I understood at a different, deeper level. Finally, the fifth time, I caught the vision of Christ's mission and His love for all people. I was so touched by my newfound understanding that I wanted to be baptized. In 1954 an American soldier baptized me and gave me the special gift of the Holy Ghost.

Dr. Paull, who had in the meantime returned home, adopted me and invited me to come live with him in the United States. I was eighteen when I joined my new family. Because I had had little formal education in Korea, I had to start with a GED test in order to receive a high school diploma. From a high school diploma to a Ph.D. was a long, hard road for me. During my educational struggles, I communicated constantly with the Lord, seeking His help and trying to discipline my life by practicing the principles I had learned from the lives of the prophets in the Book of Mormon. I was especially influenced by Nephi's strong faith and trust in the Lord and Alma's indefatigable courage in doing what is right. The Lord blessed my efforts so that I not only finished my education but also served a mission in Japan between 1957 and 1959. He has continued to bless my life with a wonderful family, material comforts, and many opportunities to serve both in His kingdom and in the world throughout the ensuing years.

Now, as a mission president in my native land of Korea, I continue to rely upon the verses in the Book of Mormon to inspire me and my missionaries to magnify our callings. I still find my greatest joy and the sustaining meaning of my life and its suffering in my testimony.

"That's What Drew Me to Him"

ELAINE CANNON

Gary, a dentist whose quarters were right next to a new tenant/dentist in a professional complex in Arizona, said, "Ralph Walker seemed nice enough when he moved in, though I wasn't unduly interested until two months later when I tried to give him a bottle of champagne for a neighborly Christmas gift at the office. He was gracious, but instead of saying he was on the wagon or something he simply explained that liquor was against his family values, though he surely appreciated my thoughtfulness. He gave me a plate of his wife's home-baked cookies! I told my wife about this, and she said that people at the school where she teaches said that you can always tell a Mormon because they don't drink or smoke and they give you cookies to start a friendship."

Ralph quickly built a solid practice of dentistry and soon had more patients than he could handle, so he referred some to Gary. . . . He continued, "The busy years pushed on, our families grew up, and one day my wife took dangerously ill. The doctors were puzzled and I was distraught. During a lunch break one day I talked with Ralph about this. We had been cordial at the office, and I had long before quit any drinking because of Ralph's example and our own growing family. Now I sought him as a wise friend for advice about my wife. His family had been through some rough times but seemed to cope with all this with equanimity. Now I was threatened and didn't know how to deal with it, so I said to him, 'Ralph, as far as I can tell from outward behavior, you and I are really not all that different. Neither of us uses tobacco or liquor. We are honest in our dealings with our fellowmen and [are] good citizens who go to the polls and cast a conservative vote. Now, why am I so out of control about my wife's problem and you seem to have survived all kinds of heartbreak? What is the difference in us—is it your religion or what?'"

The answers Ralph gave to Gary's questions about the meaning of life and what there was to look forward to after death totally changed Gary's attitude. Gary said that he should have asked Ralph about his religion years before, because from that moment of conversation his life began to change. This led to having the Mormon elders give a blessing to his wife. Gary explained, "Marcie got better—lived for nearly seven years more! It was awesome. Ultimately we both joined the Church and went to the temple a few years before she died. Our married children, too, are now studying the gospel in the way the Mormons teach it. I am so thankful for the example of Ralph. That's what drew me to him. He didn't force his religion on me, he just quietly went about his life. . . . He knew more about the purpose of life than anybody I had met before."

"Some Remarkable Influence"

CHARLES DICKENS

Editor's note: On June 4, 1863, famed British author Charles Dickens boarded the Amazon, *an America-bound ship carrying Latter-day Saints emigrating from England, with the intention of writing an exposé on this much-maligned, enigmatic people. The following account is taken from his observations.*

I go aboard my emigrant ship. . . . But nobody is in an ill-temper, nobody is the worse for drink, nobody swears an oath or uses a coarse word, nobody appears depressed, nobody is weeping, and down upon the deck in every corner where it is possible to find a few square feet to kneel, crouch, or lie in, people, in every unsuitable attitude for writing, are writing letters.

Now, I have been in emigrant ships before this day in June. And these people are so strikingly different from all the other people in like circumstances whom I have ever seen, that I wonder aloud, "What would a stranger suppose these emigrants to be!"

The vigilant bright face of the weather-browned captain of the *Amazon* is at my shoulder, and he says, "What, indeed! The most of these came aboard yesterday evening. They came from various parts of England in small parties that had never seen one another before. Yet they had not been a couple of hours onboard, when they established their own police, made their own regulations, and set their own watches at all the hatchways. Before nine o'clock, the ship was as orderly and as quiet as a man-of-war! . . .

"A stranger would be puzzled to guess the right name of these people . . . ," says the captain.

"Indeed he would."

"If you hadn't known, could you ever have supposed—?"

"How could I! I should have said they were in their degree the pick and flower of England."

"So should I," says the captain.

"How many are they?"

"Eight hundred in round numbers." . . . Eight hundred Mormons.

I afterwards learned that a dispatch was sent home by the captain before he struck out into the wide Atlantic, highly extolling the behavior of these emigrants, and the perfect order and propriety of all their social arrangements. . . . But I went onboard their ship to bear testimony against them if they deserved it, as I fully believed they would; to my great astonishment they did not deserve it; and my predispositions and tendencies must not affect me as an honest witness. I went over the *Amazon*'s side, feeling it impossible to deny that, so far, some remarkable influence had produced a remarkable result, which better known influences have often missed.

*T*hey Kept Their Composure

KEVIN STOKER

As a young boy growing up in Italy, Sergio Zicari had two strong desires: "One was to have a family and become a father, and the other was to serve Jesus Christ as a religious minister, but I did not want to do it as a 'profession' but as a volunteer."

When investigating religion through the years, he looked for more than a simple Sunday faith; he wanted a faith that would influence his thoughts and actions seven days a week. . . . He tried to be active in the religion of his parents, but too often came away feeling perplexed and dissatisfied. His church leaders couldn't answer his questions: "What happens to families after this life?" and "What happened to the Church organized by the Savior?" Studying the Bible elicited more questions than answers.

He attended several churches, meeting many people who seemed to be striving to follow Christ. But who was right? Which was the one true church? He became more confused yet continued to attend the church he had grown up in, serving as a youth leader. In 1970, he suggested to the priest that the parish organize a series of conferences for other Christian religions in the church's auditorium. The priest gave his approval, and Sergio contacted several religions, including two LDS missionaries living in a town eighteen miles away. What little Sergio knew about the Mormons was negative, but he still wanted to hear what the missionaries had to say. The conference proved to be the beginning of the gospel being preached in Mestre, Italy.

"During their lecture, the missionaries were insulted and mocked by the ministers from the other religions," Sergio recalls. "Nevertheless, the missionaries continued to smile and share their testimonies of the truth. The doctrines I heard that evening from the lips of the missionaries did not attract me very much, but their quietness, composure, and serenity were so great that I immediately desired to become like them."

At the end of the conference, Sergio was the only person who wanted to hear more about the Church. While listening to the first lesson, he realized the necessity of having a living prophet. The missionaries also had answers to his difficult questions. "For the first time in my life, I was learning about a church that made me think: 'I would be proud to belong to such a church and to know the people that I have so longed to meet.' I knew I must discover what made them so special, and I must try to become like them." . . .

. . . He was baptized April 22, 1972. [His fiancée] Elisabetta also joined the Church. They were later sealed in the temple and have been blessed with children.

Sergio was soon called to serve in the branch presidency. He has since been a branch president, district president, and counselor in both the mission presidency and the Italy Venice Stake. Thus the two great desires he had as a child were fulfilled in the restored gospel.

Like a Leaven

HAROLD B. LEE

I was down in Argentina recently, and a sweet sister, a convert now of a few years past, sidled up to me, and she asked, "Brother Lee, why doesn't the Church build a Mormon community where they could live away from the rest of the people of the world?"

As she asked the question, I remembered some things the Master said about the relationships we should have. He spoke a parable, you remember. He said, "The kingdom of heaven is like unto leaven, which a woman took, and hid in three measures of meal, until the whole was leavened" (Matthew 13:33). That's what He said the kingdom was to be like. That didn't sound like taking His people away in a Shangri-la away from all the rest of the people. His people were to be like a leaven, or like yeast to be placed in a lump of dough so that it could affect all who were round about.

Love

An Unsigned Letter

THORPE B. ISAACSON

I had the chance to know and interview [a certain young man] for his mission, and I had the privilege of setting him apart. I like to write to missionaries. I like to get their letters. I am sure I get more strength from their letters than they do from mine. This choice boy was sent to Australia. Some weeks ago he sent me a letter and in that letter there were a number of large bills, greenbacks, currency. I thought he took a chance sending it that way, but it was wrapped well. There were also enclosed an envelope addressed to another elder and a note to this elder. The missionary in his letter to me said, "Will you put this money and this memorandum in the enclosed envelope, put a stamp on it and mail it to this elder?" The letter to the missionary to whom the money was to be sent said about these words, "Enclosed is some money that I want you to have so that you can stay and finish your mission. Unsigned." His missionary companion's folks were having some financial difficulties. This boy had been saving a little money out of his missionary allowance, and he sent that to me to put in an envelope to send back to his companion, and he did not want him to know whence it came. Oh, what a lesson!

"Thank You for Lifting Us Up"

CARLOS E. ASAY

On one occasion I requested an elder to report to the mission home for a final interview and a farewell testimonial. He had been a faithful servant—one who had converted more than a few people during his two years of service. After receiving my notice, he called me on the telephone wondering if it would be all right for a couple he had recently brought into the Church to drive him to the mission office. I did not object as long as it was not an inconvenience or imposition to the man and his wife.

At the appointed day and hour, the missionary and his new converts arrived. I met them at the door and quickly observed the special love that existed between the missionary and the couple with whom he had shared the gospel. They talked and talked, as if both parties were loathe to say good-bye. Finally I reminded the little group that my time was limited and that we must proceed with the interview.

With tears in his eyes, the missionary shook hands with the couple and said: "Thanks so very much for bringing me down to Dallas." Very quickly the man responded in a quivering voice, "No, Elder, *thank you for lifting us up.*"

Missionary service is summarized beautifully in this one sentence—"Thank you for lifting us up." "Thank you for lifting us up from the pit of sin and helping us to come unto Christ."

"A Teacher Come from God"

BARBARA AND BRIANT JACOBS

Moana, a part-Maori girl, had difficulty identifying any reason she had been called to serve a stateside mission. She didn't have a testimony, and the unhappier she was, the more uncooperative she became. At times her [senior sister] companion, whom we'll call Sister Harmon, suspected that the only possible reason she could have accepted a mission call was to get a free trip home to New Zealand at the end of her mission.

One night the young girl and Sister Harmon found no one at home during their first hour of "dooring." Moana complained about her aching feet, the weather, and everything in general before asking, "Well, what idea do you have now?" Sister Harmon replied, "We're going home."

Once inside their apartment, Sister Harmon suggested that Moana take off her shoes, put a pillow on the floor, and sit down. Then Sister Harmon sat down beside her. Putting an arm around Moana she said, "I want you to tell me about you and how you feel inside. Tell me about the members of your family and what you think they are doing right now. Tell me about New Zealand and what you did there as a young girl."

As the night wore on, Moana not only talked of home, but she confided how little she knew of the gospel and how frightened and insecure and unloved she had been all her life. She had received a patriarchal blessing, but she had not read it for years. Suddenly Moana jumped up. "Would you like to see how easily a poi ball can be made?" "I'd love to," replied Sister Harmon, who for the first time saw sparkling eyes rather than sullen ones. Moana found a box of facial tissue and showed her companion how to form the sheets into a sturdy poi ball. Then she demonstrated the intricate arm and hand movements used when swinging the balls during a traditional Maori dance.

The next morning when Sister Harmon got up she found a radiant Moana humming "We Thank Thee, O God, for a Prophet" as she finished preparing their breakfast. Never before had she voluntarily fixed a meal. On the table was a letter to her parents asking that they send her patriarchal blessing by return mail. That night when the two sisters climbed into bed, they talked again about Moana and her hopes and desires and goals and why she should be serving a mission.

A week later Moana received a sudden transfer. After she had packed and left the apartment, Sister Harmon found a note on her bed. It read, "I don't have time to write. Just read John 3:2. I love you." Sister Harmon opened her Bible and read, "The same came to Jesus by night, and said unto him, Rabbi, we know that thou art a teacher come from God: for no man can do these miracles that thou doest, except God be with him."

With tears streaming down her cheeks, Sister Harmon fell to her knees and thanked her Heavenly Father for letting her help this lonely girl find herself. Months later Moana was recognized as one of the best missionaries in her zone.

"Why Do You Want to Go on This Mission?"

HAROLD B. LEE

I was out visiting a stake some months ago and was asked to interview some young men as prospective missionaries. I had been told by the stake president that one of the young men had, after a long period of hospitalization, recovered from a severe shell shock that he had received while in military service. As I faced this young man for the interview, I asked him, "Why do you want to go on this mission?"

He sat thoughtfully for several moments, and then he replied simply: "When I went into the service, it was the first time I had ever been away from my home. I found conditions strange. I found temptation on every side and the invitation to sin. I needed strength to keep from sin, and I went before my Heavenly Father and prayed to him in faith to give me that strength to resist evil. God heard my prayer and gave me that strength. After the period of training was over and we neared the combat area, we heard the booming of the guns that foretold the message of death that was coming over constantly. I was afraid, and I was quaking all over. I prayed to God for courage, and he gave me courage, and there came over me a peace that I had never enjoyed before. When we got over in the Philippines, I was assigned to duty as an advance scout, which meant I was ahead of the combat forces and sometimes was almost surrounded by the enemy. I knew that there was only one power in the earth that could save me, and I prayed to that power to protect me, to save my life, and God heard my prayer and returned me back to my company."

Then he said to me: "Brother Lee, I have all those things to be grateful for. It is little enough that I can do to go out now as an ambassador of Jesus Christ, to teach mankind these blessed things that I have received as a child in my home."

$\mathscr{A}$ Well-Placed Pen

KEVIN STOKER

One day back in the 1930s, Elder Louis G. Tremelling and his companion couldn't find a seat aboard a noisy bus in Buenos Aires, Argentina. As the missionaries stood near the door, Elder Tremelling watched a tall young man with an athletic build dispense bus tickets. He had a money-bag, a ticket dispenser, and a notebook attached to a clipboard for keeping a record of each transaction.

"All at once I could see he was in trouble," Elder Tremelling recalls. As he moved up for a closer look, the elder heard the young man say he had lost his pencil and would lose his job unless he kept an accurate record of his transactions.

"I don't know what impelled me to reach into my pocket and give him my new pen—which I had just purchased that day," Elder Tremelling says. He handed the pen to the ticket dispenser, explaining, "You need it more than I do."

"Who are you?" the young man asked. The Americans told him that they were missionaries from The Church of Jesus Christ of Latter-day Saints.

"Where do you live?"

They said they lived in Haedo, a small town outside of Buenos Aires.

"I live there too," was the response.

Two days later, the young man found the missionaries' residence and returned the pen. His name was Samuel Boren. Before he could leave, the missionaries asked him if he would allow them to visit his home and teach him and his family the restored gospel.

"You surely can," he said without hesitation.

Three weeks later, on September 12, 1936, he and his parents and family were baptized. Shortly after that, Samuel served a mission in Argentina. He later married Clara Angela Lorenzi.

In the years that followed, Samuel became a successful building manager for the Church in South America and for business interests in North America.

He also has helped build the kingdom. Since joining the Church, Samuel has served as a mission president in Mexico and twice in Italy. He also has been a Regional Representative.

In 1985 he was called as the first president of the Lima Peru Temple. Among those called as officiators at the temple were Louis and Isabel Tremelling from Idaho Falls, Idaho.

The Man They Had Seen
in Their Dreams

JOHN O. SIMONSEN

Editor's note: John O. Simonsen and his wife served as missionaries among the Indians at Fort Peck, Montana, in the early 1920s.

The older Indians told us, on several occasions, the story of their first meeting with Elder [Melvin J.] Ballard. They said that one day Elder Ballard was traveling east across Montana by train. As the train approached a very small town which was just being settled, Elder Ballard noticed, from the train window a huge encampment of several hundred Indians. Their teepees were pitched in a large circle on the prairie. Elder Ballard was instantly interested and felt a keen urge to visit with them. He obtained stopover privileges and left the train to spend the day at the encampment, with the intention of proceeding on his journey the next day. He hired a horse and buggy, secured an interpreter, and drove out to the Indian encampment at a place called "Chicken Hill," on the banks of the Missouri River. . . .

Elder Ballard left the horse and buggy and with the interpreter walked out among the people. As he approached them, they showed signs of great emotion and began talking excitedly to him. They seemed to be asking him for something. The interpreter explained that many of the Indians had seen, in dreams, a white man come among them. Always he had had his arms laden with books which were of great value to them. They had seen the man distribute the books and teach the Indians from their contents. As soon as they saw Elder Ballard, they recognized him as the man they had seen in their dreams and they wanted the books he was supposed to bring to them.

Of course, Elder Ballard was exceedingly impressed and told them briefly the story of the Book of Mormon and of its significance to them. He told them he must go on his way now, but that he would return soon to bring them the books and teach them more.

When Elder Ballard returned to the town he felt impressed to buy two lots in the newly-laid-out town, which he obtained for a very low price. When he returned a short time later the lots had skyrocketed in price to such a figure that he was able to sell them at a tremendous profit. The money thus obtained was used to buy building materials and some acreage further out of the town, in fact, at "Chicken Hill." There a boarding school and a chapel were built, and the Lamanites were given their Book of Mormon and were taught the Gospel, as well as general school work. Many of the Indians joined the Church there, and today their descendants and many others are firm in the faith. Great spiritual manifestations occurred in this particular place, as the writings of Elder Ballard relate. Many were the healings, and many the spiritual gifts that were made manifest among the Indians because of the faith Elder Ballard instilled into them.

One such instance was told to us by an Indian called "Looking." He was a young boy when Brother Ballard came among his people, and he had been blind since birth. When he heard that there was a "Mormon Prayer Man" (as the Indians called the missionaries) on the reservation, he begged to be taken to Elder Ballard that he might be blessed to receive his sight. Elder Ballard administered to him, and through the power of the priesthood and the child's simple, sincere faith, his sight was restored and he was appropriately given the name of "Looking." In gratitude, Looking insisted on giving the hay from his small field each year to help feed the Church livestock at Chicken Hill.

One reason for their great love for this exceptional man was that he visited with them in their simple little log huts without pride or pretence. He would drop in on a family and say, "Now,

Sister Black Dog, don't you put on any special fuss for me." (As if they could, with their very primitive living conditions.) "We will just sit here on the floor and visit together and eat whatever you have ready." To hear them tell of this great man visiting with them in their humble abodes and eating their simple and sometimes strange food, and to see their eyes light up with love when telling about it, was inspiring to us.

"Aren't You a Member?"

ROBERT E. WELLS

My friend had finished his first year at college, spent the summer at home in the West, and now was back at school and on his way to church the first Sunday of the new school year. After getting off the bus and walking quickly up the street towards the chapel several blocks away, he noticed that he was overtaking a slower-walking young man about his same age, wearing cowboy boots and a dark suit. The member didn't recognize him from the previous year and assumed he was a member from the West looking for the chapel.

Overtaking the newcomer just in front of the chapel, and in an open and friendly way, my friend greeted the newcomer. "New student at the university?" The young man nodded. "Where are you from?" my friend asked. The reply was Montana or Wyoming, I believe. Putting his arm around the newcomer's shoulders, my friend said, "Well, come on in, brother. I'll introduce you to everyone." They went inside, introductions were exchanged, and the sacrament meeting proceeded normally.

When it was time to go to priesthood meeting, my friend asked the new fellow, "What priesthood do you hold?" "What?" he asked, a bit bewildered. "Yeah, priest or elder?" "What are you talking about?" was the innocent response. My friend, much surprised, exclaimed, "Aren't you a member?" "Not of this church," was the answer. "I was just looking for my own church further up the street when you invited me in." My friend was confused. "But you sang bass in the hymns." "Yeah," was the answer. "I can read music. I heard others singing parts. Wasn't I supposed to?" "But you took the sacrament," continued my friend. To which the young man replied, "Everyone else was doing it. I'm a Christian too. Wasn't I supposed to join you?"

The newcomer was baptized in a short time. He had found instant friendship, brotherhood, and love. He felt the spirit of the meeting. After his baptism he admitted that what most caught his attention was the lay leadership of nonprofessional preachers and teachers going about Sunday worship as though that was the way it was supposed to be. Furthermore, the simplicity of the sacrament every Sunday administered by young men serving God in a sweet and innocent way impressed him tremendously. And the members' acceptance of him as one of them from the first moment he entered the door indicated to him that they enjoyed the love of God in their lives.

My friend told me, "Had I known out in the street that he was not a member, I might have done something wrong. I might have said, 'You wait here. I'll go get the missionaries.' Or I might have said, 'You wait here. I'll go get a Book of Mormon and convert you with it.' Those ideas would surely have frightened him away. But I did the right thing unknowingly. I just treated him like a member, invited him in, introduced him to everyone as 'Brother,' and everyone else accepted him immediately."

The Spirit of Missionary Service

CARLOS E. ASAY

Several years ago I received an assignment to attend a conference in the eastern part of the United States. I made the proper arrangements with the expectations that all would go according to my well-laid plans. But when the day of departure arrived, everything seemed to come unraveled, and I boarded the airplane with a sagging spirit and in a less than congenial mood.

I took my assigned seat on the plane, opened my briefcase, and began to work on some materials that required careful review. It pleased me to observe that the seat next to mine was not occupied. This raised my hopes of traveling undisturbed by idle conversation with some stranger.

Just moments before the boarding gate was closed, a very hairy and unkempt young man rushed through the doorway, swept by the flight attendants, and took the only remaining seat—the one next to mine. I must admit that this turn of events annoyed me. Not only had I lost the privacy I wanted, but I was now crowded next to a person who appeared worldly, smelled of oil and grease, and seemed eager for conversation.

I ignored the intruder and continued with my reading. I even turned obliquely in my seat away from the man, hoping that the positioning of my body would send a signal that might keep him at bay.

Once the airplane was off the ground and had reached its flying altitude, my unwelcomed traveling companion turned to me and said, "I fear that I may have offended you, and I want to explain why I look so grubby." He then explained that he was from New York and had been attending an auto mechanics seminar in Utah—a seminar that concluded with a hands-on workshop. He further explained that the workshop concluded only a few minutes before the time of departure from Salt Lake City and that he had not been provided the time to change clothes, wash, and make himself more presentable. He concluded by saying, "I hope that you will forgive me for the way I look and smell."

Oh, how very ashamed I was! Ashamed that I had prejudged a man; ashamed that I had been so selfish in my desires and behavior; and ashamed that I had carried a spirit so contrary to my calling.

I introduced myself and apologized for my aloofness. He accepted my apology graciously. Soon we were engaged in a conversation wherein we both talked about family, church, and other important things. Eventually we opened the scriptures and discussed the restored gospel with an openness usually reserved for old friends. Upon arrival at our destination, we parted company with a warm handshake and the promise that he would receive representatives of the LDS Church, whom I would send.

I shall never forget the swing of mood and the change in spirit that came over me as I pushed aside my own selfish interests, became genuinely interested in a very fine young man, and began to share with him my faith in God. This experience served to remind me that we should not prejudge others despite outward appearances. It also reminded me that when we live outside of ourselves and attempt to share the gospel of Jesus Christ with others, a beautiful spirit comes into our presence. It is the spirit of testimony, the spirit of the scriptures, and the spirit of brotherhood that hover over and around all honest missionary efforts.

Courage

$\mathcal{S}$peaking Up

GEORGE D. DURRANT

Editor's note: As president of the Kentucky Louisville Mission, George D. Durrant regularly wrote "newsletters" to instruct, encourage, and inspire the missionaries over whom he presided. This story is taken from one of his newsletters.

I saw a young man at McDonalds. He was eating a hamburger, and I, a Big Mac. His hair was short and he wore a white shirt and tie. I came within a gnat's eyelash of saying: "Hi, there. I was wondering if you are a Mormon missionary."

He would have said, "No, I'm not."

Then I'd have said, "Well, you sure look like an Elder in the Mormon Church."

"Do I?"

"You sure do. You look like a real winner, and that's the way they look."

"Well, thanks for the compliment."

"Anyway, I'm a Mormon missionary. What do you know about the Mormons?"

"Not much."

"Seeing as how you look like a missionary, I'm going to have two of them come by your home and see you. What's your address?"

And then the Elders would have taught him, and then he'd have been baptized and his wife and her parents and her uncle. And this man's sons would have gone on missions and . . . But all of this won't happen because I only *thought* of saying something.

Then I thought I'd better eat my Big Mac and keep my thoughts to myself.

Now, as I think back, I feel terrible. I wish I could be back there at McDonalds and have a second chance. But I can't go back. I feel sad that I missed it. I humbly pray that I'll never miss such an opportunity again.

What about you? You deserve to give someone a break today at McDonalds. Don't miss your opportunity to build a golden arch from someone to the truth.

My First Sermon

HENRY G. BOYLE

Never shall I forget the first time I was called upon to make an effort to preach the gospel. It was in Pittsylvania County, Virginia, in the month of June, 1844.

I had been ordained an Elder and set apart to take a mission to Virginia, in company with Elder Sebert C. Shelton.

My extreme youth prevented me from realizing the responsibilities of a mission. Being a beardless boy, it never occurred to me that I would be called upon to preach. Up to that time I never had been upon my feet to say a word in public.

At a meeting which had been advertized for two weeks, at the Methodist camp meeting ground, in a grove, in the County before mentioned, were gathered an assemblage of six or seven hundred men, women and children, priests, doctors and lawyers, the largest meeting I had ever witnessed up to that time.

I came to this meeting from one part of the County, and Elder Shelton was expected to come from another quarter. But the time to commence meeting had arrived, and Elder Shelton had not.

The audience was impatient. A party of three or four of the leading citizens waited upon me, to know if I would not address the meeting. There never had been a "Mormon" meeting in that County before, and they could not afford to be disappointed.

I was sitting near the center of the meeting (not realizing that the stand was my place) when these men made the inquiry.

If a battery of artillery had been discharged in our midst, I do not think it would have so startled me, as did this request.

For the first time I began to realize that it was my duty to try to advocate the religion I professed.

Just as I was going to answer that I would make an effort, Elder Shelton walked upon the stand, and this seemed to lift a mountain from my shoulders.

Brother Shelton looked wearied and sick, but opened the meeting with singing and prayer, and sang again before he discovered me in the audience. Then he immediately called upon me to come to the stand and preach, as he was too sick and feeble to attempt it.

To say I was scared, would scarcely convey a proper idea of my condition. I was in a tremor from head to feet, and shook like a leaf in a storm, scarcely knowing what I did.

I took up Elder Shelton's Bible which lay upon the front board, and without any premeditation, I opened at the third chapter of John, and read the fifth verse.

By the time I had finished reading, all my trembling had left me, and I felt as calm and collected as the quiet that succeeds the storm. The subjects of the first principles of the gospel were opened to me like print, only plainer and more powerful.

Faith, repentance, baptism for the remission of sins and the laying on of hands for the reception of the Holy Ghost, came to me in succession and in their order. And those priests, doctors, lawyers and people did not appear to me more formidable than so many butterflies.

No miracle ever performed by the power of God, could have had a more convincing effect upon me, than did the help that came to me through the power of the Holy Ghost on that occasion. And I am fully convinced in my own mind that never since have I preached a more effective discourse, nor one accompanied by more of the power of God.

$\mathscr{A}$ Younger Brother's Courage

MICHAELENE P. GRASSLI

Eleven-year-old Shane stood in testimony meeting and bore his testimony. At the conclusion he said, "Brothers and sisters, I know the gospel is true, and when I grow up I want to be a missionary and tell everyone that the gospel is true so they can be happy. I pray for Cory [his older brother] that he will repent, that he will stop doing what he is doing wrong, and that he will prepare himself to be worthy to serve a mission."

Those of us in the congregation were in awe at Shane's courageous declaration. We wondered what would happen.

A year and a half later, at his missionary farewell, Cory said, "I have had several people ask me what made me decide to go on a mission. It's because a year and a half ago I was sitting in testimony meeting with my family, and I didn't take the sacrament. Shane noticed that, and when he bore his testimony, he challenged me to repent and prepare for a mission. I thought, if Shane wants to go on a mission and he's watching me as his example, I have to live up to what he expects of me. The courage of my little brother made me want to go on a mission and gave me the courage to change so I could."

$\mathcal{D}$aniel Spencer's Conversion

ANDREW JENSON

Until 1840 no Elder of the Mormon Church had preached in [Daniel Spencer's] native town. The late John Van Cott, however, belonged to the same region, and already his relatives, the Pratts, had been laboring to impress Mr. Van Cott with the "Mormon" faith. But Daniel Spencer, up to this date, had no relationship whatever with the people with whom himself and his brother Orson afterwards became so prominently identified. At this time Daniel Spencer belonged to no sect of religionists, but sustained in the community the name of a man marked for character and moral worth. It was, however, his custom to give free quarters to preachers of all denominations. The "Mormon" Elder came; and his coming created an epoch in Daniel Spencer's life. Through his influence the Presbyterian meeting house was obtained for the "Mormon" Elder to preach the gospel, and the meeting was attended by the elite of the town. At the close of the service the Elder asked the assembly if there was any one present who would give him "a night's lodging and a meal of victuals in the name of Jesus." For several minutes a dead silence reigned in the congregation. None present seemed desirous to peril their character or taint their respectability by taking home a "Mormon" Elder. At length Daniel Spencer, in the old Puritan spirit and the proud independence so characteristic of the true American gentleman, rose up, stepped into the aisle, and broke the silence: "I will entertain you, sir, for humanity's sake." Daniel took the poor Elder, not to his public hotel, as was his wont with the preachers generally who needed hospitality, but he took him to his own house, a fine family mansion, and the next morning he clothed him from head to foot with a good suit of broad cloth from the shelves of his store. The Elder continued to preach the new and strange gospel, and brought upon himself much persecution. This produced upon the mind of Daniel Spencer an extraordinary effect. Seeing the bitter malevolence from the preachers and the best of the professing Christians, and being naturally a philosopher and a judge, he resolved to investigate the cause of this enmity and unchristianlike manifestation. The result came. It was as strongly marked as his conduct during the investigation. For two weeks he closed his establishment, refused to do business with any one, and shut himself up to study; and there alone with his God he weighed in the balances of his clear head and conscientious heart the divine message and found it not wanting. One day, when his son was with him in his study, he suddenly burst into a flood of tears, and exclaimed: "My God, the thing is true, and as an honest man I must embrace it; but it will cost me all I have got on earth." He had weighed the consequences, but his conscientious mind compelled him to assume the responsibility and take up the cross. He saw that he must, in the eyes of friends and townsmen, fall from the social pinnacle on which he then stood to that of a despised people. At mid-day, about three months after the poor "Mormon" Elder came into the town of West Stockbridge, Daniel Spencer having issued a public notice to his townsmen that he should be baptized at noon on a certain day, took him by the arm and, not ashamed, walked through the town taking the route of the main street to the waters of baptism, followed by hundreds of his townsmen to the river's bank. The profoundest respect and quiet were manifested by the vast concourse of witnesses, but also the profoundest astonishment. It was nothing wonderful that a despised "Mormon" Elder should believe in Joseph Smith, but it was a matter of astonishment that a man of Daniel Spencer's social standing and character should receive the mission of the Prophet and divinity of the Book of Mormon. The conversion and conduct of Daniel Spencer carried a deep and weighty conviction among many good families in the region around, which, in a few months, resulted in the establishment of a flourishing branch of the Church.

6,000 Miles to Bring a Message

DEAN HUGHES AND TOM HUGHES

One day [Elder Hugh B. Brown] was going door to door in Norwich, England. He knocked on a door and received no answer. Through an open window he saw a woman sitting in her living room, knitting. He knocked again, but she still didn't answer. What he didn't know was that she had spotted him, recognized that he was a Mormon missionary, and decided not to go to the door.

But Elder Brown was not so easily ignored. He wanted her to hear what he had to say. So he walked around her house and knocked hard, with his walking stick, on the back door. Needless to say, the woman flew to her door and gave the missionary quite a talking to. Elder Brown later wrote:

> When she did stop, I said, "My dear lady, I apologize for having annoyed you, but our Heavenly Father sent me 6,000 miles to bring you a message, and inasmuch as he sent me I can't go home until I give you that message."
>
> "Do you mean the Lord sent a message to me?" she asked.
>
> "I mean just that," I answered. "He sent me because he loves you."
>
> "Tell me the message."

After telling her the story of Joseph Smith and the restoration of the gospel to the earth, he apologized again for disturbing her. Then he added, "Sister, when you and I meet again, and we will meet again, you are going to say, 'Thank you, and thank God that you came to my back door and insisted on speaking to me.'"

Ten years later, Hugh Brown was in England again, this time as a soldier in World War I. A conference was scheduled in Norwich, but the mission president was sick and couldn't attend. He called Major Brown to see if he could go fill in. He did so willingly. At the end of the meeting, a woman came up to see him. Tears rolled down her cheeks as she kissed his hand. She said:

> I do thank God that you came to my door ten years ago. When you left that day, I thought about what you had said. I couldn't get it out of my mind. I was fighting it, but I couldn't sleep that night. I kept thinking, 'God has sent a message to me.' . . . I tried to find the missionaries from the address on the tract you left, and when I found them, you had returned to Canada. We continued to investigate until my daughter and I joined the Church.

Elder Brown was deeply touched, and he remembered all the doors he had knocked on during his mission—and all of the rejections. He wondered whether other people he had taught had later accepted the gospel.

I'll Go Where You Want Me to Go

MARY BROWN

It may not be on the mountain height
Or over the stormy sea,
It may not be at the battle's front
My Lord will have need of me.
But if, by a still, small voice he calls
To paths that I do not know,
I'll answer, dear Lord, with my hand in thine:
I'll go where you want me to go.

Perhaps today there are loving words
Which Jesus would have me speak;
There may be now in the paths of sin
Some wand'rer whom I should seek.
O Savior, if thou wilt be my guide,
Tho dark and rugged the way,
My voice shall echo the message sweet:
I'll say what you want me to say.

There's surely somewhere a lowly place
In earth's harvest fields so wide
Where I may labor through life's short day
For Jesus, the Crucified.
So trusting my all to thy tender care,
And knowing thou lovest me,
I'll do thy will with a heart sincere:
I'll be what you want me to be.

I'll go where you want me to go, dear Lord,
Over mountain or plain or sea;
I'll say what you want me to say, dear Lord;
I'll be what you want me to be.

".Are You a Mormon?"

JOSEPH FIELDING SMITH

Editor's note: At the age of fifteen, Joseph F. Smith served a mission to the Hawaiian Islands, where he labored for nearly four years. The following experience took place in California as he traveled home to Salt Lake City.

It was while on this homeward journey that [Joseph F. Smith] was forced to pass through a very trying scene. It should be understood that the feeling existing towards the Latter-day Saints was running very high. The terrible scene at Mountain Meadows was fresh in the minds of the people, and of course they erroneously blamed President Brigham Young in particular, and all of the "Mormon" people of being guilty of that horrible deed. Then, also, the army of the United States was on its way to Utah by orders from the President of the United States, their coming being based upon false charges that had been made by government officials from Utah who were extremely antagonistic against the Latter-day Saints. There were many men scattered abroad who had murder in their hearts and who said they would not hesitate to kill "Mormons" wherever they were found. Under these circumstances the members of the Church were forced to travel in small companies on their journey homeward bound. One day after the little company of wagons had traveled a short distance and made their camp, a company of drunken men rode into the camp on horseback, cursing and swearing and threatening to kill any "Mormons" that came within their path. It was the lot of Joseph F. Smith to meet these marauders first. Some of the brethren when they heard them coming had cautiously gone into the brush down the creek, out of sight, where they waited for this band to pass. Joseph F. was a little distance from the camp gathering wood for the fire when these men rode up. When he saw them, he said, his first thought was to do what the other brethren had done, and seek shelter in the trees and in flight. Then the thought came to him, "Why should I run from these fellows?" With that thought in mind he boldly marched up with his arms full of wood to the campfire. As he was about to deposit his wood, one of the ruffians, still with his pistols in his hands and pointing at the youthful Elder, and cursing as only a drunken rascal can, declaring that it was his duty to exterminate every "Mormon" he should meet, demanded in a loud angry voice, "Are you a 'Mormon'?"

Without a moment of hesitation and looking the ruffian in the eye, Joseph F. Smith boldly answered, "Yes, siree; dyed in the wool; true blue, through and through."

The answer was given boldly and without any sign of fear, which completely disarmed the belligerent man, and in his bewilderment, he grasped the missionary by the hand and said:

"Well, you are the _____ _____ pleasantest man I ever met! Shake, young fellow, I am glad to see a man that stands up for his convictions."

Joseph F. said in later years that he fully expected to receive the charge from this man's pistols, but he could take no other course even though it seemed that his death was to be the result. This man, evidently the leader of the band, then rode off, the others following him, and the Mormon company was not molested further. It was a tense moment, nevertheless, and the company thanked the Lord for their safe deliverance.

⒯he Greatest Thing in Life

WALLACE F. TORONTO

A young Ukrainian, Tarnawskyj by name, who had been studying for the ministry in the Greek Catholic Church, was on his way from Warsaw, Poland, to New York City, there to attend a graduate school for the ministry of that church. He came by the way of the city of Prague. As he was going down the street he saw the sign, "Church of Jesus Christ of Latter-day Saints." He noticed that we were holding a meeting at that time. He thought to himself: "I have learned of those people in my studies. I am curious. I think I will go in and see what they have to say."

He entered, dressed in his black robe and white collar, and sat in the back. He was a young man about twenty-eight or thirty years of age. Two of our missionaries stood up and explained some of the principles of the Gospel. They bore their testimonies. Since he spoke Ukrainian, which is kindred to Czech, he understood them. After the meeting he came up and asked: "When do you hold the rest of your services?" We enumerated the meetings of the week and he came to all of them, even including the Relief Society. In a few weeks he made this request: "Brother Toronto, I would like to be baptized into this Church." . . .

. . . Continuing, he said: "I have found the most priceless thing in all the world. I want the Gospel of Jesus Christ. I have been seeking it for years in the universities and the divinity schools of many lands, and I have never found anything that can equal this."

I said: "All right. As soon as we instruct you a little more fully in the Gospel we shall be happy to have you as a member of the Church." He was subsequently baptized. Upon accepting baptism a great characteristic of truth took hold of him, that of wanting to tell somebody else about it. Of course, those he thought of first were his loved ones back in Poland. He wrote them a long letter, in which he declared: "I have found the greatest thing in life. I want to tell you something of the Gospel of Jesus Christ, that you, too, might enjoy the blessings which flow from it."

I met him a few days later. He wore a long face and was very dejected. "What on earth has happened to you, Brother Tarnawskyj?" "I just received a letter from my folks in Poland. They tell me here 'Dear Son and Brother: If you do not immediately renounce this thing you call Mormonism we shall cease to send you one penny of support, which you know is your only means of livelihood; and furthermore, we shall disown you as a son and a brother!'"

"What is your answer, Brother Tarnawskyj? You are at the cross-roads. You have a grave decision to make."

"Oh, Brother Toronto, you know what my answer is: 'Dear loved ones, I cannot renounce the thing I hold dearest in life, the Gospel of Jesus Christ. I pray God that you, too, at some future time, through my efforts or the efforts of others, might also come into this Church.'"

From that day until this, so far as I know, he has not received one penny or one word from his people. He found himself in Czecho-Slovakia, a foreigner, unable to secure employment.

During these troublesome times the subtle political forces in Central Europe had operated to break down the Czecho-Slovakian Republic, so that Slovakia gained its freedom, as well as the little province of Ruthenia or Sub-Carpathian Russia, far to the east, hardly larger than the County of Salt Lake. Brother Tarnawskyj finally proposed: "Brother Toronto, many of my countrymen are out there in Ruthenia, a large group of Ukrainians among whom I could work. Since I am an educated man, I think I could get a position as an Inspector in the Ministry of Education. Can you help me get there? I want to become a self-sustaining citizen." "All right. We will help you get to Ruthenia, if you think you can succeed."

Upon his arrival in this new autonomous state, he filed his application for a position in the ministry. It went through the various hands and much red tape through which such things have to pass and finally reached the Minister himself. Up to this point all went well. When it reached the Minister there was great delay. Finally our brother wrote me a letter and said: "Brother Toronto, I don't know what the trouble down here is. I am qualified for the position, and I have pulled every string I know. And I have prayed. The Lord God knows I am hungry. He knows I need a place to rest my head. I have tried to live the Gospel since I joined the Church. From the earnings on little jobs I have secured here and there I have set aside my tithing, and as soon as the mails go through I will send it on to you. Why, oh why does the Lord persecute me like this?" But in conclusion he added: . . . "Perhaps it is all for the best."

A card came a few days later: "I am going to take a job out in the little town of Perecyn as a humble school teacher, where I can make enough to at least buy me a few crusts of bread."

He was employed there for three days, when that tiny state of Central Europe, Sub-Carpathian Russia, was drenched in blood by the Hungarian hordes which swept over it. Men, women and children by the hundreds were left dying in the streets. He and nine of his Ukrainian companions were routed out of bed at five o'clock one morning and thrown into prison. After twenty-four hours of intense suffering they were called before a military court consisting of one man in the uniform of a Hungarian officer. He had the sole right to say, "You live," or "You die." The ten men came before him. They were asked two questions: "How long have you been in this country?" and "What is your religious affiliation?"

Our brother led the others. To the first question he replied that he had been there so and so many weeks. "What is your religious affiliation?"

"I am a member of the Church of Jesus Christ of Latter-day Saints. Sometimes they call us 'Mormons.'"

"Mormons? Mormons? I have heard of you folks. I have read

of you in the newspapers of Budapest. I hear your people have done some good in this world." A tense moment of hesitation and then, "You go free."

His nine companions came up after him. They were asked the identical questions. Being no more guilty than he himself, they were nevertheless condemned to death, and shot down in cold blood before the sun went down that day.

This brother finally got out of the country, and wrote me another letter. "Brother Toronto," he said, "I know the Lord does move in a mysterious way His wonders to perform. The Gospel is the most priceless thing I have in the world. I know the Lord has preserved my life, that I may be a beacon light to my fellow men. He has not only preserved my life, in the way I have described to you, but He has also protected me, for had I received the position of Inspector in the Ministry of Education I today would have been sitting in the concentration camps of Hungary, subjected to some of the most terrible torture known to humankind. I owe all I have to the Gospel of Jesus Christ."

*T*he Frog's Reply

AUTHOR UNKNOWN

In the year 1845, I was appointed on a mission from Nauvoo, to labor about Cass County, Illinois, in company with Theodore Curtis.

After traveling together we concluded to separate, and I continued alone, preaching wherever an opportunity presented itself.

One evening I was approaching a little town called Virginia, foot-sore and weary, having been frequently denied food. . . .

Towards evening I found a number of persons congregated at the country store. I saluted them with "Good-evening," and inquired the opportunity of getting a chance to preach in that place. . . .

. . . I was soon assured by one or two that there was no earthly show for a "Mormon" preacher to be heard in that place.

I replied, "I would like to preach in that nice, newly-finished meeting-house just opposite." A man spoke up quite authoritatively, and said that no "Mormon" should preach in that house, which had just been dedicated—I think for Presbyterian worship.

They termed this man the deacon. This produced considerable talk, for many of the crowd were of what is termed the liberal or infidel persuasion, so much so that the deacon was overwhelmed by argument, shame and reproach, for refusing a boy like me a chance to preach. . . .

He remarked, "Your people believe in laying hands on the sick; don't you?"

I answered that we did, and because Christ had said in His remarkable commission to His apostles, that this was one of the signs following, quoting Mark xvi., 15–18. I also quoted James v., 14.

"Yes, yes;" says he, "that is all very good, but that says only once, and your Elders sometimes lay hands twice in succession on the same person. Whoever heard of Jesus or the apostles doing anything like that?" He then cited an instance where, as he said, Joseph Smith had done this in administering to a sick woman.

The good-natured excitement was intense. The deacon thought I was overwhelmed, and proposed that if I could prove a similar transaction from the scriptures, I might preach in that house that very night.

Eagerness now seized the men, and the deacon chuckled over his presumed victory, and boasted of his acquaintance with the "Blessed Word."

I unbuckled my valise, drew forth my little Bible, and opened it intuitively to this passage in Mark viii., 22–25: "And he cometh to Bethsaida; and they bring a blind man unto him, and besought him to touch him. And he took the blind man by the hand, . . . and put his hands upon him, and asked him if he saw aught. And he looked up, and said, I see men as trees, walking. After that he put his hands *again* upon his eyes, and made him look up: and he was restored, and saw every man clearly."

The reading of this scripture; the sudden finding of it, for I was led to it as clearly as a man leads his horse to the water; its aptness and conclusiveness, accompanied by the jeers of the infidel portion of the crowd, mortified the deacon—he was discomfited.

I remarked that I would, according to the deacon's terms, preach in the church that evening, provided some one would find candles. The candles were instantly offered, and accordingly, I preached with power and the demonstration of the Spirit.

After the close of the services, I found a resting place with one of the most avowed infidels of the neighborhood, who had listened to the talk between the deacon and myself, and who particularly enjoyed the good man's discomfiture. By his persuasion I staid some time in the neighborhood, occupying occasionally the school-house.

He even proffered me some land to build me a house if I would stay, preach and teach school; but my mind was bent on returning to Nauvoo.

But one evening, when I had been preaching my intended farewell sermon in the closely-packed school-house, and just at its close, a person arose and said that, God willing, he would deliver a discourse there the next Sunday, and expose the "Mormon" delusion, giving his announcement all the force and emphasis possible.

My friends gathered at my place of stopping, and, joining with my host, prevailed upon me to stay. The word was given out that I had gone to Nauvoo.

At the time appointed a great crowd had convened—time, early candle-light.

I arrived late, purposely. My friend and I took seats near the door.

The preacher, after preliminaries, opened the Bible, and, for his text, read the 13th and 14th verses of the 16th chapter of Revelations.

After dilating upon the swampy nature of the soil contiguous to Nauvoo, styling it a good place for frogs, and facetiously comparing it to the "mouth of the dragon," he came down heavily on the "false prophet," the miracles, etc. It was a most scathing rebuke on "Mormonism."

His final peroration was on the habits of the frogs, which, while no footsteps were heard, croaked and croaked, but at the first sound of an approaching footstep, dodged their heads beneath the water. "So," said he, at the same time rising to the sublime height of his oratory, "where, oh where is the frog that croaked here a day or two ago? Gone to that slough of iniquity, Nauvoo, the seat of the dragon and the false prophet. Why has he fled? Because he heard the footsteps of your true shepherd." After much interlarding, he dismissed by prayer.

I immediately arose and said that the frog was there yet, and would croak once more, naming the time.

Shouts from the audience named that same evening as the time, and the reverend preacher, amid jeers, cheers and cries of, "Give the boy a chance!" made for the one door.

My friend was alive to the emergency, and I, nothing loth, opened a fusillade from I. Timothy, 4th chapter, while the preacher was hemmed in by the crowd, and my friend with his back to the door.

After an exhaustive testimony of the work, we all departed, some pleased, some chagrined.

"God Had Broken the Bands of Fear"

GEORGE Q. CANNON

The first time the writer was called upon to speak to a mixed congregation of Saints and inquirers he was in the company of nine Elders. There were only two or three of them who had ever spoken in public; but as he was the youngest of the party, and felt that he was but a boy, he thought they would all be called upon before him. To his surprise, however, the Elder who was presiding called first upon him.

True to his resolve, he arose and commenced. For two or three, or probably five minutes, he did pretty well. Then he got confused, his ideas were in a jumble, and he forgot all he ever knew. If the bottom had dropped out of his memory, it could not have been worse. He sat down, feeling a little ashamed; but not discouraged. He was on a mission, and he was determined not to back down and fail. But it is very mortifying to get up to speak and then break down. . . .

After this, circumstances required him to go out among the people alone. . . . The feeling of dread was terrible. He had been in places of peril where life was in danger; but he never felt as he did about preaching. He was alone and a stranger, and among a strange people. But he would not shrink. He knew that the gospel was true, that he had the authority to preach it, that the people had to be warned, and, therefore, with all his fear, he could not hold his tongue. He felt like Paul did when he said to the Corinthians: "Woe is unto me if I preach not the gospel."

About six weeks after he commenced his ministry alone two messengers arrived from a distant town to invite him to come there and preach. They had heard about the doctrine he taught, and the people he had baptized, and they wanted to learn more about the principles. He returned with the messengers. A large meeting house was obtained in which to preach. It was crowded, for the people had never before had the privilege of hearing a sermon delivered by a Latter-day Saint. You can imagine how he felt. Here was a people anxious to hear, and yet how weak he was, and how full of fear and trembling! When he arose to give out the hymn the sound of his voice in that large building scared him. Then he prayed, and afterwards gave out another hymn. He had called mightily upon God for help. When he commenced to speak the Spirit of the Lord rested upon him as it never had done before. The people had faith, and their hearts were prepared to receive the truth. For upwards of an hour he spoke, and he was so carried away in the Spirit, that he was like a man in a trance. Joy filled his heart and the hearts of the people. They wept like children, and that day was the beginning of a good work in that place.

I shall not attempt to describe to you the gladness that our young missionary felt. He had been a slave; but now he was free. God had broken the bands of fear, and he felt to glorify Him for His goodness.

Full-Time Missionaries

Obedience

GEORGE MACDONALD

I said: "Let me walk in the fields."
   He said: "No, walk in the town."
I said: "There are no flowers there."
   He said: "No flowers, but a crown."

I said: "But the skies are black;
   There is nothing but noise and din."
And He wept as He sent me back—
   "There is more," He said; "there is sin."

I said: "But the air is thick,
   And fogs are veiling the sun."
He answered: "Yet souls are sick,
   And souls in the dark undone!"

I said: "I shall miss the light,
   And friends will miss me, they say."
He answered: "Choose tonight
   If I am to miss you or they."

I pleaded for time to be given.
   He said: "Is it hard to decide?
It will not seem so hard in heaven
   To have followed the steps of your Guide."

I cast one look at the fields,
   Then set my face to the town;

He said, "My child, do you yield?
Will you leave the flowers for the crown?"

Then into His hand went mine;
And into my heart came He;
And I walk in a light divine,
The path I had feared to see.

$\mathscr{L}$etters to Home

ANN CREBS WEIGHT

Editor's note: The following excerpts are taken from letters Ann Crebs wrote to home while serving in the Thailand Bangkok Mission in 1983 and 1984.

$\mathbf{M}$ay 2, 1983

I have never wished that I had not come more than today. I am so frustrated. I hate it here. And to think we do the same thing over and over *every* day. I want to go home so badly. I feel now that it would be easier to go home with all the embarrassment than to stay. I am so miserable. My feet, the heat, the language. NEVER before has a year and a half seemed so *long*. It seems an ETERNITY. What have I done??? I can hardly believe it will ever end. I don't see right now how I will *ever* enjoy it.

May 9, 1983

I am *constantly* thirsty. The kitchen is outside of the house. I *hate* to go in there. It is moldy and full of various bugs. We have a huge "dug gaa" thing that looks like a minicrocodile that goes in there every evening and makes really loud noises. This place reminds me of the scripture where it talks about "every creeping and crawling thing that walked the earth," or however it goes. I had to stop wearing lip gloss because the bugs stick to my lips. The heat is so intense that I feel I can't breathe.

We have to take "dipper" showers. We just dip out water from a barrel and pour it down our bodies. OOOHHH. No matter how hot it gets, I can't quite get used to that cold water running down my back.

I went to the branch for the first time yesterday. I was totally blown away. I didn't understand one thing that was said. There were about twenty people there including missionaries. They meet in a house. . . . I could NOT believe that missionaries have been coming to Chiang Mai for *years* and there are only twenty people at church to show for it.

The MTC was a picnic compared to this. It was a struggle. This seems an impossibility. I am on the verge of crying at *all* times. It's hard to see the light ahead. I can't understand one thing that is said to me. I'm sure the people wonder how I can ever teach them anything when I can't even talk. *Please* put my name in at the temple and pray for me.

May 16, 1983

You have never seen conditions like those in Thailand. . . . Some Thais have little stands on the streets and then live above them, but there are millions who just live in little shacks. They sit around or sleep all day in the dirt. Most of the shacks have one whole open side and lots of bugs!

We went to the market today and I nearly threw up. You wouldn't believe it. They have the scariest looking things to eat and the smells are so nauseating! PLEASE!!! SEND ME FOOD OR I WILL DIE out here.

I'd do just about anything to come home. I find myself wishing I would just get hit by a bus and get hurt bad enough to go home but not die.

May 23, 1983

Well, they tell you not to be negative in your letters home but I feel like being honest with you so you can really see what it is like. I just don't see how I'll ever make it. HELP! It's funny, I had to talk you guys into my serving a mission and now you have to talk me into staying! I have never felt so alone. I am still *really* struggling, but it has forced me to rely on the Lord more because there is no one else. I know if I ever learn the language I will owe it all to Him.

June 6, 1983

A mission can be a really good thing if that's what I decide. I can mope around and feel sorry for myself or get out there and work, put my all into it, and know I did the best I could. I figure if I'm going to be here and serve the Lord, I don't want to do it halfheartedly.

July 1, 1983

Something that really helped me this past week was reading in Alma where he is feeling terrible because everyone was rejecting him and not showing interest in his message. The Lord told him to cheer up and be happy because he was doing what he was supposed to and keeping the commandments (8:15). Another one was Alma 26:27: "Now when our hearts were depressed, and we were about to turn back, behold, the Lord comforted us, and said: . . . bear with patience thine afflictions, and I will give unto you success." Boy, am I holding on to that one!

August 8, 1983

I am getting caught up in the work now and am actually enjoying it a bit. We were riding our bikes out in a total rainstorm and had 15 miles to go. It was like a rain blizzard, and we were SOAKED. Some girls motioned to us and had us stand under their porch for a while—they were so concerned about us. Then a man stopped on his motorcycle and gave me his rain poncho. We offered to pay him or to return it later, but he said no. Then he disappeared into the distance. I am really growing to love these people!

We went to the hospital to see Tawn Tip, our investigator who was sick and had received a blessing from the elders, but she had already gone home! So we went to her house. As soon as she saw us, tears began to stream down her face. She grabbed on to me and hugged me and cried and testified of the power of the blessing the elders had given her. By then we were all crying and my heart was full of love for her and the fact that I had played a small part in such a miracle. I thought about that on the way back home and realized that I do have something to offer, that I can be an instrument for the Lord, even if I am struggling and can't understand. I felt so encouraged.

I can't believe I am saying this, but I LOVE OUR BRANCH! . . . When I first came, I was appalled, but now I can see that we are actually lucky. We have some good members, very few, but they keep things above water.

September 16, 1983

I have developed such a love for the Thai members. My new companion (a Thai) has sacrificed so much to be here. . . . They don't have a separation of state and religion in Thailand, so when people convert, you are not only asking them to change religions but also to give up so many of their traditions and holidays. It is too overwhelmingly embarrassing to their parents, so they disown their children who convert in order to save face. My companion, like so many others, has come out here to serve for 18 months with no love and no support.

October 25, 1983

I want to take back all those things I said about the Thai people! Thai people are SO neat! . . . You can learn so much from them. In a lot of ways, they're better than Americans. They really are a hard-working people, too. Sometimes during the day you might see them sleeping under their houses, but that's because they start work at 4:00 or 5:00 in the morning to avoid the midday heat. I have such a love for them, and they also seem to care for me. . . . Once you look past all the unpleasant things of Thailand, you are left with wonderful, loveable people.

November 21, 1983

Yesterday we had a GREAT baptism in the new font at the church. I was so proud. . . . She has been the neatest investigator and I just LOVE her. She will make a *great* member and will really help the branch out. "Oh, how great shall be your joy." It's greater than anything I have ever experienced. Some days this seems such a small price to pay for such inexpressible joy.

March 20, 1984

My new companion is SO frustrated. She can't believe we just stand at street boards for hours, but I taught her the wonderful lesson I have come to learn—that after the trial of our faith come the miracles. And boy have they come. We stood for three days straight with barely a nibble and were so tempted to give up—it sure would have been easier. But we stuck it out and sure enough, on the fourth day, we received THREE referrals, and ONE WAS A FAMILY!!! We were so excited and felt blessed for our diligence.

August 9, 1984

I am being a missionary to its fullest, and I LOVE it. . . . I just don't know how I can leave here—really. I know a year and a half ago I was on the other side of the world saying the same thing! OH! I've come so far and learned so much since then. At home I was just another face in the crowd—here I feel I am making an important contribution. . . . I wake up each morning and I say, "Okay, today I am going to hang on to every minute," and the next thing I know, it has passed and is gone from my reach forever. . . . A year and a half ago I would have DIED to be home hanging out and cruising around. Now all I can think about is how much I am needed here and all the work there is still to do. I have been so blessed.

Love,
Ann

"*I* Didn't Really Know"

GEORGE D. DURRANT

I was standing in the service station where I worked. I excitedly told my boss, "I'm going on a mission."

He was a little shocked at first, but then he spoke: "I'm glad you are going. It is better than college. It is better than the army. You'll learn so much. When you get home, you'll be more confident. You will be able to meet people better. You'll be able to speak and to lead."

He then jokingly added, "We'll miss you." As he said this, his mood changed and he continued, "There is just one thing I'd like you to promise me."

I asked, "What's that?"

He replied quickly and with a bit of emotion. "When you get home, don't stand up and say that you know the Church is true."

He paused as we looked into each other's eyes. Then he continued: "There is no way you can know that, George. You are honest and so I know that you won't lie. All those who say that they know the Church is true are liars. I don't go to church because of all those who stand up and say that. There is no way that they can know."

He concluded by saying: "George, you'll do great. But remember, you are honest. Don't come home and say that you know the Church is true because neither you nor anyone else can know that."

The joy I had felt with the bishop went out of me and doubt crept in. I didn't really *know* the Church was true. I hoped it was. I did know that prayers were answered and I knew that there was a God, but beyond that I didn't know. . . .

I quickly picked up the language there in England and started to give it my all. I had so much to learn. Most of the eight I came out with had been student body leaders. Others in the mission possessed many noteworthy attributes. And there I was in the midst of all of them.

I wasn't a speaker, I wasn't a scholar, I wasn't a great athlete. I didn't really even have a testimony. And most of all I was deeply frightened.

I recall that my first prayer in England occurred when the ship was docking. My prayer was prompted by the thought, "Could I possibly swim home?" I prayed, "Oh, dear Father, just give me the strength to go ashore."

And starting with such a humble beginning and with so little to qualify me for the work, I became the greatest average missionary to ever serve in England. . . .

But after the excitement of going was over, then came the discouragement of being there. After a month or so . . . I again began to wonder about trying to swim home. A series of events were disturbing and discouraging.

My bike (sold to me by another Elder) wasn't as good as he said. It was extremely difficult to pedal, and the generator wouldn't generate. . . .

Word also came that Elder Matthew Cowley, my spiritual hero, had died.

I didn't get any Christmas presents from home.

My landlady, whom I had come to love because she reminded me of my mother, became desperately ill.

I wasn't learning the discussions very fast and had about decided I could never learn so much.

Our investigators weren't too anxious to investigate.

I caught a cold (I only had one cold on my entire mission but it lasted for two years).

Finally, after a month or so it was Christmas day and I cannot ever recall being so depressed. We didn't have Christmas dinner where we lived because of the landlady's illness. And I was too near pneumonia to venture out into the fog to go to a member's house.

Stripped of all the things I had come to associate with Christmas, I was indeed down in the mouth.

I sat looking into the glowing coal embers of a warm fire. Out of the corner of my eye I saw my Bible. Almost subconsciously I reached over and picked it up. Opening it to the book of Matthew, I began to read. My mind gradually shifted away from my troubles and sorrows. I began to focus my thinking on the glorious mission of the Savior. On that Christmas day I walked with him. In my mind I could see him heal the sick, encourage the sinner to repent, criticize the hypocrites, comfort the sorrowful. I saw him walk on the water, and hold the children in his arms. I agonized with him in the garden and watched him die on the cross. I felt a surge of hope as I witnessed him rise from the tomb.

I've never had such a Christmas. I spent it with him.

A few nights later I had a dream about him and about my relationship to him. I don't think I'll ever be the same again because of that dream.

I then knew that he was indeed the Savior of the world. My testimony was firmly forming.

A month or so later my district president asked me to give a talk in a forthcoming missionary meeting on the subject of Joseph Smith.

The other Elders had taken their turns and each had deeply impressed me. I wanted to do as well. I was fearful that I'd forget and not be able to speak with any fluency.

I studied with more intensity than I'd ever done before. I prayed for the ability and courage to speak with clarity and power.

Finally the time arrived. We, nine other Elders and myself, were assembled on the front two rows of the little Hull chapel.

I stood to speak. My fear was soon replaced by other emotions. Something seemed to be happening deep inside my soul. I said, "And in response to Joseph Smith's prayer, God the Father and his Son Jesus Christ appeared to him."

When I said that, I felt a feeling that made me begin to cry. I tried to go on but I could not. I looked down at the floor and I sobbed. Finally, I was able to gain some control. I looked into the faces of my companions. They too were in tears. I was then able to speak again. I told of the persecution and the martyrdom of the Prophet.

I then sat down. But I was not the same person who had stood up, for now I *knew*. I knew that the message I was proclaiming was true. I knew that The Church of Jesus Christ of Latter-day Saints was indeed what its name says—the Lord's church. It is my belief that on that day in England I became a man.

$\mathcal{H}$is Testimony Was Simple and Direct

DEAN HUGHES AND TOM HUGHES

B. H. Roberts was called . . . to the Northern States Mission . . . and that spring he boarded a train for the midwest. He was asked to establish missionary work in the area of Sioux City, Iowa. An experienced missionary, William Palmer, would remain a few days with him in the area, and then, at least for a time, Elder Roberts would be on his own.

The two missionaries got off a train in Omaha, Nebraska, and immediately had a chance to teach a group of investigators who were already being taught by other missionaries. Elder Palmer, a man of considerable experience, spoke to the group first. He preached on and on about a complicated gospel theory he had developed, but those in the audience were not impressed.

When B. H. Roberts was called on to speak, it was his first chance ever to preach the gospel to people outside the Church. He was frightened and confused. But when he arose to speak, he thought of Joseph Smith's first vision and the events that followed. Elder Roberts gave the account simply and directly, then bore his testimony. He felt a response from the Spirit, and he continued to preach. On the following morning, six of the people in the meeting asked for baptism.

To My Missionary Son

GAY N. BLANCHARD

My fledgling has flown
Half the world round—
Far out of reach of my lullaby's sound . . .
Far past the edge of a wild warning cry . . .
Far beyond sight of my hungering eye.

How can I share my warm cloak of care?
Wrap him in love in that far other where?
Gratefully, Father, I thank thee
For prayer.

Take on its wings the thread of my strength
And bind him secure in its infinite length.
Let its sure pulse keep a rhythm between
That sings of my faith in him, steady, serene.
Bring through its channels his message to me . . .
That our hearts may be one
In dimension with thee.

ℐhe Golden Contact

KEVIN STOKER

Near the end of January 1985, Sister Dzidra Yallouris, a fifty-nine-year-old single missionary serving in the Arkansas Little Rock Mission, fervently prayed to be led to a "gold contact." . . .

In a few days her prayer was answered. While proselyting where the Spirit prompted them to go, she and her companion, Sister Marilyn E. Cooper, were led to a home in Jonesboro, Arkansas. "We knocked on the door, and a smiling, gracious woman opened it and said, 'Come in,'" Sister Yallouris recalls. "It seemed as if she had expected us."

The missionaries taught the first discussion and made an appointment to return. As they were leaving, the investigator said, "I want to be baptized."

"This lady, Rosemary Andrews, had been prepared by the Lord for the gospel," Sister Yallouris says. "Within a week we gave her all the discussions. She received them with an open heart and mind, and she believed it. The Spirit was strong while we were teaching her."

The baptismal date was set for February 9, 1985. On February 7 the sisters visited Rosemary and discovered that some evangelists had called her and warned her not to join the Mormon church. They said that they were coming to see her and tell her all about the Mormon religion and its doctrine. . . .

First to walk in was a large woman. . . . She packed a worn Bible under her arm. The evangelist was followed by her husband and another woman. . . . "My companion and I looked at each other, and our hearts sank to our heels. I began to pray silently, pleading to the Lord for help. 'Oh, Heavenly Father, what must we do? How will we face this lady and her companions? They most likely know the Bible very well and will try to talk Rosemary out of joining the Church. Oh, please help us, Heavenly Father.'"

As she prayed, Sister Yallouris felt her fear replaced by a sweet, calm feeling. Her companion opened the discussion with prayer and had barely said "Amen" when the evangelist began telling Rosemary why she shouldn't join the Church.

"Suddenly," Sister Yallouris says, "the large lady stopped talking. She shut her eyes and tried to open her mouth, but no sound came out. She was grasping for words. A Christlike love filled my heart, and I began to talk. I told them about my conversion. I told them about the gospel and the restored Church. The man even asked a few questions. I finished by bearing my testimony."

All the while Sister Yallouris talked, the evangelist frantically tore through the pages of her Bible, trying to find a scripture. The sisters taught for more than two hours, and the large woman's frustration grew as she continued to rustle through her scriptures. Finally, Sister Yallouris asked her what scripture she wanted to find. She said Galatians 1:6–12. The missionary helped the evangelist find the passage, which happened to be the same one the missionaries had read to Rosemary the day before.

Sister Yallouris asked the evangelist to give a closing prayer, and she accepted. After she finished praying, she scooped up her Bible and quietly departed. From the beginning, Rosemary had watched and listened to the spectacle in silence. Now she and the missionaries marveled at the way the Lord had answered their prayers. Two days later Rosemary was baptized and confirmed a member of The Church of Jesus Christ of Latter-day Saints.

Sanctified by Service

CARLOS E. ASAY

I'll never forget an experience I had in Australia a few years ago. My wife and I had been invited to participate in a mission conference. As a part of that conference program, some missionaries sang and testified. One of the participants was a young man who had a special glow upon his face. In fact, my wife observed, "I've never seen anyone sparkle with the truth as he does."

When the meeting finished, before I could even leave the stand this young man said, "Elder Asay, may I speak with you?"

I turned to the mission president and said, "Do you mind if I speak with this young man?"

He said, "Oh no, be my guest."

I said to the young man: "Go down to the bishop's office and wait; I'll be there shortly." He turned and walked down the aisle.

When he was out of earshot, I turned back to the mission president and asked, "Do you suppose there's a problem here?"

His response was, "Couldn't be. He's a living legend already in this mission."

At the bishop's office, the missionary was so conscious of my time that he wouldn't even let me sit down. He said, "Elder Asay, you have forgotten me, haven't you?"

"Yes, I guess I have," I admitted. "Please forgive me."

Then he said, "Several years ago I came to your office with my bishop and stake president. I came because I had done many foolish things in high school, I had made myself unworthy of my priesthood, and I required some special clearance before I could serve. In fact, you may recall that when I gave you a listing of my transgressions, you said, 'I will never allow you to serve.'"

Then I remembered. I remembered that his sins were so reprehensible to me that I had said, "No, you can't serve!" He pled, his bishop pled, and his stake president pled for special consideration. Finally I relented by saying, "You may serve on two conditions: first, that you live every commandment strictly; and second, that you will seek to become the best missionary in your assigned mission."

He said, "Elder Asay, it thrilled me to know that you were coming to this mission. Next week I go home, and I just wanted to report that for two years now I haven't stretched or bent or broken a single rule or commandment."

"God bless you for that," I responded.

And then he added, "I may not be the best missionary in this mission, but I'm awfully close."

I thanked him for his wonderful report. He walked to the door, turned back, and added, "Elder Asay, for the first time in many, many years I feel perfectly clean."

I said, "You are. You have been sanctified by your service. Now, please go home and don't lose what you have gained."

*M*issionary Miracles

MARY ELLEN EDMUNDS

When I was serving as a missionary, I thought that if I worked hard enough, prayed with enough faith, and did the best I could, Big Miracles would happen. I think I wanted to be able to write a journal entry something like this:

"One day we got up, and we were prompted to eat rice for breakfast, and then we felt we should go tracting, and then we saw some clouds in the sky that formed a house number, and we went there, and a family was sitting in their living room dressed all in white, waiting for us, and they had their tithing in a powdered milk can, and they'd had a dream, and we were in the dream, and they recognized us immediately, and we started telling them about Joseph Smith, and the wife burst into tears because her great-great-great-grandmother had found a Joseph Smith tract in the Old Country as she was digging up her yams, and it was in her tribal language, which, incidentally, is not one of the ninety-eight languages in which the tract is currently printed . . ."

Well, that didn't happen to me. But before I became a missionary I thought it likely would. I had listened to many missionaries give their homecoming messages, and when two years' experiences are condensed into twenty minutes, you hear of some wonderful miracles. I found that missionary work is *work*— hard work, hour by hour, day by day—and that even though I prayed for people with all my heart, things didn't always work out the way I hoped. And yet I have seen many miracles, and I am awfully glad I kept journals on my missions, because you don't always know when you're at the beginning of, or in the middle of, or at some other part of a miracle. There's not always a loud voice announcement from heaven: "Here it comes! This is it!" Miracles are usually quiet, wonderful, and easily missed.

The Shoes

ARDETH GREENE KAPP

Upon our arrival in the mission field, we quietly asked several individuals, "Who do you think are the extra-mile missionaries?" Although several different names were given, without exception [one] young man . . . would always be mentioned. You can be sure we were anxious to meet him.

In just a day or two we met this young elder. He was a fine-looking young man, but not particularly outgoing or dynamic, as one might suppose. When we learned more about him, we became aware that things had not always turned out the way he had hoped. He had perhaps not participated in as many baptisms, not always had totally obedient companions, and not always experienced the sunshiny days he might have hoped for; in fact, there seemed to be a lot of rain in his life.

There are many, many disappointments that go with missionary work and with life, but this young man always seemed to have a vision of what could be. He worked with a hope that was relentless. His hope allowed him to see more than others could see. He was always well-groomed and happy, and even though it was near the end of his mission, when even the best-cared-for white shirts begin to show signs of many washings, he still looked good and his shoes were always shined.

One day he was in the office writing a quick note, kneeling by a desk because no chair was immediately available. I walked into the room and my eyes became riveted on the soles of his shoes. "Elder," I said, "tell me about your shoes." He smiled and stood up quickly, covering the evidence of his worn-out soles. "What are you going to do with those shoes when you return home?" I asked him. With a big smile, he told me he was going to trash them. He saw no value in them. They were completely worn out; even the cardboard that had been used to cover the large holes in the bottoms was worn through.

Yes, they were thoroughly worn out, but to me their value was far greater than it had been when they were new. "Elder," I asked, "will you give me your shoes?" He looked quite surprised, but agreed that I could have his shoes with the soles that had been worn through in the sacred labor of saving souls. He asked me what I intended to do with them, and I told him I was going to keep them and in twenty years or so, if I was still around, I was going to present them to his son or daughter who would be filling a mission and say to him or her, "Walk in the steps of your noble father."

Sources and Permissions

The Restoration and the Book of Mormon

"The Morning Breaks, the Shadows Flee" by Parley P. Pratt, from *Hymns of The Church of Jesus Christ of Latter-day Saints* (Salt Lake City: The Church of Jesus Christ of Latter-day Saints, 1985), no. 1.

"'I Felt Such a Desire to Read the Book'" by Mary Lightner, as quoted in Jay A. Parry and others, eds., *Best-Loved Stories of the LDS People,* vol. 2 (Salt Lake City: Deseret Book Company, 1999), pp. 391–93.

"'A Very Strange Book'" by Parley P. Pratt, from *Autobiography of Parley P. Pratt* (Salt Lake City: Deseret Book Company, 1938), pp. 18–22.

"Dmitry the Believer Finds a Book" by Howard L. Biddulph, from *The Morning Breaks: Stories of Conversion and Faith in the Former Soviet Union* (Salt Lake City: Deseret Book Company, 1996), pp. 80–82.

"'Do You Ever Cry When You Read the Book of Mormon?'" by Marion G. Romney, from Conference Report, April 1949, p. 41.

"The Voice of God Again Is Heard" by Evan Stephens, from Jack M. Lyon and others, eds., *Best-Loved Poems of the LDS People* (Salt Lake City: Deseret Book Company, 1996), pp. 291–92.

"'What Is That Book?'" by Kevin Stoker, from *Missionary Moments* (Salt Lake City: Bookcraft, 1989), pp. 123–24.

"The Cheapest Book in the Store" by Robert E. Wells, from *Hasten My Work* (Salt Lake City: Bookcraft, 1996), pp. 23–24.

"'Burn the Book'" by Don Vincent di Francesca, from the *Improvement Era*, May 1968, pp. 4–7.

Faith and Prayer

"A Prayer for Five Shillings" by Amasa Potter, from *Labors in the Vineyard* (Salt Lake City: Juvenile Instructor Office, 1884), pp. 80–81.

"Valentina's Faith" by Howard L. Biddulph, from *The Morning Breaks: Stories of Conversion and Faith in the Former Soviet Union* (Salt Lake City: Deseret Book Company, 1996), pp. 124–25.

"Led by the Spirit" by John D. Whetten, from *Making the Most of Your Mission* (Salt Lake City: Deseret Book Company, 1981), pp. 38–39.

"First Prayer" by Dean Hughes and Tom Hughes, from *We'll Bring the World His Truth* (Salt Lake City: Deseret Book Company, 1995), pp. 64–67.

"He Is Breathing His Last!" by Eliza R. Snow Smith, from *Biography and Family Record of Lorenzo Snow* (Salt Lake City: Deseret News Company, 1884), pp. 65–66.

"Welcome and Welcome!" by Rendell N. Mabey and Gordon T. Allred, from *Brother to Brother* (Salt Lake City: Bookcraft, 1984), pp. 1–7.

"A Prayer for a Font of Water" by Grant H. Taylor. Previously unpublished.

"'How Shall I Know?'" by Jacob Hamblin, from James S. Little, *Jacob Hamblin* (Salt Lake City: Bookcraft, 1969), pp. 3–5.

"Real Intent" by Elder "C," from Margie Calhoun Jensen, ed., *When Faith Writes the Story* (Salt Lake City: Bookcraft, 1973), pp. 44–46.

Workings of the Spirit

"Benbow Farm" by Wilford Woodruff, from *Leaves From My Journal* (Salt Lake City: Juvenile Instructor, 1882), pp. 77–82.

"Vera's Dream" by Howard L. Biddulph, from *The Morning Breaks: Stories of Conversion and Faith in the Former Soviet Union* (Salt Lake City: Deseret Book Company, 1996), pp. 98–99.

"A Sermon from a Blank Text" by Theodore B. Lewis, from *A String of Pearls* (Salt Lake City: Deseret Book Company, 1882), pp. 44–46.

"'I Had Never Preached in My Life'" by Claudius V. Spencer, from *Labors in the Vineyard* (Salt Lake City: Juvenile Instructor Office, 1884), pp. 13–15.

"'The Gain and the Joy Are All Mine'" by Marion D. Hanks, from *Bread upon the Waters* (Salt Lake City: Bookcraft, 1991), pp. 258–60.

"A Living Testimony" by Melvin S. Tagg, from *The Life of Edward James Wood: Church Patriot* (unpublished master's thesis, Brigham Young University, 1959), pp. 22–24.

"'I Was Truly Astonished'" by Susan Easton Black, from Susan Easton Black, ed., *Stories from the Early Saints Converted by the Book of Mormon* (Salt Lake City: Bookcraft, 1992), pp. 12–14.

"He Was Speaking Words Which He Did Not Understand" by Anthon H. Lund, from Edwin F. Parry, ed., *Sketches of Missionary Life* (Salt Lake City: George Q. Cannon & Sons Company, 1899), pp. 59–61.

"Found Twice by the Spirit" by Howard L. Biddulph, from *The Morning Breaks: Stories of Conversion and Faith in the Former Soviet Union* (Salt Lake City: Deseret Book Company, 1996), pp. 86–88.

"My Brother's Conversion" by Heber J. Grant, from Conference Report, October 1922, pp. 188–90.

Conversion and Testimony

"A Remarkable Conversion" by LeGrand Richards, from *Missionary Experiences* (Salt Lake City: Bookcraft, 1975), pp. 305–6.

"'This Is Why I Joined the Church'" by Kenneth W. Godfrey, from H. Wallace Goddard and Richard A. Cracroft, eds., *My Soul Delighteth in the Scriptures* (Salt Lake City: Bookcraft, 1999), pp. 108–9.

"The Road to Sharon" by Albert C. Cooper, from Hartman and Connie Rector, ed., *No More Strangers,* vol. 4 (Salt Lake City: Bookcraft, 1990), pp. 118–22.

"Like a Little Child" by Marion D. Hanks, from *Bread upon the Waters* (Salt Lake City: Bookcraft, 1991), pp. 311–13.

"Reunited by the Gospel" by Howard L. Biddulph, from *The Morning Breaks: Stories of Conversion and Faith in the Former Soviet Union* (Salt Lake City: Deseret Book Company, 1996), pp. 91–93.

"A Lesson in Humility" by Eldred G. Smith, from Conference Report, April 1955, p. 42.

"First Visit of the Missionaries" by Janet Cathery-Kutcher, from Barbara B. Smith and Shirley W. Thomas, comp., *Where Feelings Flower* (Salt Lake City: Bookcraft, 1992), p. 44.

"A Testimony of Tithing" by LeGrand Richards, from Preston Nibley, comp., *Missionary Experiences* (Salt Lake City: Bookcraft, 1975), pp. 310–11.

"A Spaniard Finds the Truth" by Kevin Stoker, from *Missionary Moments* (Salt Lake City: Bookcraft, 1989), pp. 169–70.

"'I Would Give Everything I Own to Prove You Wrong'" by Lucile C. Tate, from *LeGrand Richards: Beloved Apostle* (Salt Lake City: Bookcraft, 1982), pp. 44–46.

"The Dryland Mormon" by Franklin D. Richards, from *The Challenge and the Harvest* (Salt Lake City: Deseret Book Company, 1983), pp. 94–95.

"He Didn't Dare Send Anyone Else" by Wilford Woodruff, from *Leaves from My Journal* (Salt Lake City: Juvenile Instructor, 1882), pp. 80–81.

Divine Protection

"Evacuation from Germany" by Dean Hughes and Tom Hughes, from *We'll Bring the World His Truth: Missionary Adventures from*

Around the World (Salt Lake City: Deseret Book Company, 1995), pp. 49–52.

"Rescued by Strangers" by Kevin Stoker, from *Missionary Moments* (Salt Lake City: Bookcraft, 1989), pp. 31–32.

"The Time Is Far Spent" by Eliza R. Snow, from *Hymns of The Church of Jesus Christ of Latter-day Saints* (Salt Lake City: The Church of Jesus Christ of Latter-day Saints, 1985), no. 266.

"He Commanded the Waves to Be Still" by Henry D. Taylor, from Conference Report, October 1970, pp. 19–20.

"The Lord's Blessings" by Amasa Potter, from *Labors in the Vineyard* (Salt Lake City: Juvenile Instructor Office, 1884), pp. 75–78.

"Delivered from the Evil One" by Wilford Woodruff, from *Leaves from My Journal* (Salt Lake City: Juvenile Instructor Office, 1882), pp. 48–49.

"My Pocket Bible" by Lorenzo Snow, from Eliza R. Snow Smith, *Biography and Family Record of Lorenzo Snow* (Salt Lake City: Deseret News Company, 1884), pp. 37–38.

"'Wicked Men Can't Sing like Angels'" by George Albert Smith, from *The Teachings of George Albert Smith: Eighth President of The Church of Jesus Christ of Latter-day Saints,* ed. Robert and Susan McIntosh (Salt Lake City: Bookcraft, 1996), pp. 23–24.

"'Your God Is a God of Power'" by Kevin Stoker, from *Missionary Moments* (Salt Lake City: Bookcraft, 1989), pp. 27–28.

Member Missionaries

"'My Courage Was Put to a Test'" by Anita R. Canfield, from *By Small and Simple Things* (Salt Lake City: Bookcraft, 1999), pp. 70–71.

"The Shoemaker Bears His Testimony" by John A. Widtsoe, from *In the Gospel Net: The Story of Anna Karine Gaarden Widtsoe* (Salt Lake City: Bookcraft, 1966), pp. 63–69.

"Brightly Beams Our Father's Mercy" by Philip Paul Bliss, from *Hymns of The Church of Jesus Christ of Latter-day Saints* (Salt Lake City: The Church of Jesus Christ of Latter-day Saints, 1985), no. 335.

"'Saturday Is Fine'" by Robert E. Wells, from *Hasten My Work* (Salt Lake City: Bookcraft, 1996), pp. 38–39.

"Every Day She Would Go to the Market" by Spencer W. Kimball, from *Proclaiming the Gospel: Spencer W. Kimball Speaks on Missionary Work,* ed. and arr. Yoshihiko Kikuchi (Salt Lake City: Bookcraft, 1987), p. 250.

"The Only Phone on the Block" by Robert E. Wells, from *Hasten My Work* (Salt Lake City: Bookcraft, 1996), pp. 13–14.

"The Governor's Copy of the Book of Mormon" by George Albert Smith, from *Story Gems,* comp. Albert L. Zobell (Salt Lake City: Bookcraft, 1953), pp. 23–26; adapted from Conference Report, October 1950, pp. 175–78.

"The Best Years" by Anita R. Canfield, from *A Perfect Brightness of Hope* (Salt Lake City: Deseret Book Company, 1991), pp. 97–99.

Reactivation

"A Plea for Those Who Err" by Henry A. Tuckett, from Jack M. Lyon and others, eds., *Best-Loved Poems of the LDS People* (Salt Lake City: Deseret Book Company, 1996), p. 190.

"'We Are Here to Welcome You into the Ward'" by Anita R. Canfield, from *A Perfect Brightness of Hope* (Salt Lake City: Deseret Book Company, 1991), pp. 92–93.

"The Prodigal Cowboy" by Robert E. Wells, from *Hasten My Work* (Salt Lake City: Bookcraft, 1996), pp. 72–77.

"A Delinquent Elder" by Ezra Taft Benson, from *God, Family, Country: Our Three Great Loyalties* (Salt Lake City: Deseret Book Company, 1974), pp. 186–88.

"Spiritual Rehabilitation" by Lucile C. Tate, from *LeGrand Richards: Beloved Apostle* (Salt Lake City: Bookcraft, 1982), pp. 111–12.

"Brother Clay" by Anita R. Canfield, from *Remember, and Perish Not* (Salt Lake City: Bookcraft, 1998), pp. 76–80.

"'Can You Be Worthy for Ten Minutes?'" by Marvin J. Ashton, from *What Is Your Destination?* (Salt Lake City: Deseret Book Company, 1978), pp. 42–43.

"Other Sheep I Have" by William Cullen Bryant, from Jack M. Lyon and others, eds., *Best-Loved Poems of the LDS People* (Salt Lake City: Deseret Book Company, 1996), p. 290.

"'Do You Know That Feeling?'" by Anita R. Canfield, from *A Perfect Brightness of Hope* (Salt Lake City: Deseret Book Company, 1991), pp. 115–16.

Example

"'Who Taught You the Gospel?'" by Harold B. Lee, from *The Teachings of Harold B. Lee: Eleventh President of The Church of Jesus Christ of Latter-day Saints,* ed. Clyde J. Williams (Salt Lake City: Bookcraft, 1996), pp. 590–91.

"'I Can't Figure You Out'" by Kevin Stoker, from *Missionary Moments* (Salt Lake City: Bookcraft, 1989), pp. 69–71.

"Your Own Version" by Paul Gilbert, from *Best-Loved Poems of the LDS People,* ed. Jack M. Lyon and others (Salt Lake City: Deseret Book Company, 1996), pp. 75–76.

"'The Fifth Time through I Saw Christ's Mission'" by Paull Hobom Shin, from Eugene England, ed., *Converted to Christ through the Book of Mormon* (Salt Lake City: Deseret Book Company, 1989), pp. 70–72.

"'That's What Drew Me to Him'" by Elaine Cannon, from *Count Your Many Blessings* (Salt Lake City: Bookcraft, 1995), pp. 115–16.

"'Some Remarkable Influence'" by Charles Dickens, from *The Uncommercial Traveller* (London: Chapman & Hall, 1907), pp. 200–211.

"They Kept Their Composure" by Kevin Stoker, from *Missionary Moments* (Salt Lake City: Bookcraft, 1989), pp. 48–49.

"Like a Leaven" by Harold B. Lee, from *The Teachings of Harold B. Lee: Eleventh President of The Church of Jesus Christ of Latter-day Saints,* ed. Clyde J. Williams (Salt Lake City: Bookcraft, 1996), p. 588.

Love

"An Unsigned Letter" by Thorpe B. Isaacson, from Conference Report, April 1965, pp. 126–27.

"'Thank You for Lifting Us Up'" by Carlos E. Asay, from *The Seven M's of Missionary Service* (Salt Lake City: Bookcraft, 1996), p. 96.

"'A Teacher Come from God'" by Barbara and Briant Jacobs, from *Missions for Marrieds* (Salt Lake City: Deseret Book Company, 1983), pp. 29–31.

"'Why Do You Want to Go on This Mission?'" by Harold B. Lee, from *The Teachings of Harold B. Lee: Eleventh President of The Church of Jesus Christ of Latter-day Saints,* ed. Clyde J. Williams (Salt Lake City: Bookcraft, 1996), p. 592.

"A Well-Placed Pen" by Kevin Stoker, from *Missionary Moments* (Salt Lake City: Bookcraft, 1989), pp. 153–54.

"The Man They Saw in Their Dreams" by John O. Simonsen, from *Melvin J. Ballard . . . Crusader for Righteousness* (Salt Lake City: Bookcraft, 1966), pp. 55–57.

"'Aren't You a Member?'" by Robert E. Wells, from *Hasten My Work* (Salt Lake City: Bookcraft, 1996), pp. 35–36.

"The Spirit of Missionary Service" by Carlos E. Asay, from *The Seven M's of Missionary Service* (Salt Lake City: Bookcraft, 1996), pp. 7–8.

Courage

"Speaking Up" by George D. Durrant, from *Get Ready! Get Called! Go!* (Salt Lake City: Bookcraft, 1979), pp. 65–66.

"My First Sermon" by Henry G. Boyle, from *A String of Pearls* (Salt Lake City: Juvenile Instructor Office, 1882), pp. 64–65.

"A Younger Brother's Courage" by Michaelene P. Grassli, from *What I Have Learned from Children* (Salt Lake City: Deseret Book Company, 1993), p. 66.

"Daniel Spencer's Conversion" by Andrew Jenson, from *Latter-day Saint Biographical Encyclopedia* (Salt Lake City: Andrew Jenson History Company, 1901), p. 287.

"6,000 Miles to Bring a Message" by Dean Hughes and Tom Hughes, from *We'll Bring the World His Truth: Missionary Adventures from Around the World* (Salt Lake City: Deseret Book Company, 1995), pp. 40–41.

"I'll Go Where You Want Me to Go" by Mary Brown, from *Hymns of The Church of Jesus Christ of Latter-day Saints* (Salt Lake City: The Church of Jesus Christ of Latter-day Saints, 1985), no. 270.

"'Are You a Mormon?'" by Joseph Fielding Smith, from *Life of Joseph F. Smith: Sixth President of The Church of Jesus Christ of Latter-day Saints* (Salt Lake City: Deseret News Press, 1938), pp. 188–89.

"The Greatest Thing in Life" by Wallace F. Toronto, from Conference Report, April 1940, pp. 53–55.

"The Frog's Reply," author unknown, from *Fragments of Experience* (Salt Lake City: Juvenile Instructor, 1882), pp. 9–12.

"'God Had Broken the Bands of Fear'" by George Q. Cannon, from *My First Mission* (Salt Lake City: Juvenile Instructor Office, 1882), pp. 10–11.

Full-Time Missionaries

"Obedience" by George MacDonald, from Jack M. Lyon and others, eds., *Best-Loved Poems of the LDS People* (Salt Lake City: Deseret Book Company, 1996), pp. 295–96.

"Letters to Home" by Ann Crebs Weight, adapted and expanded from Dean Hughes and Tom Hughes, *We'll Bring the World His Truth: Missionary Adventures from Around the World* (Salt Lake City: Deseret Book Company, 1995), pp. 75–79.

"'I Didn't Really Know'" by George D. Durrant, adapted from *Get Ready! Get Called! Go!* (Salt Lake City: Bookcraft, 1979), pp. 13–19.

"His Testimony Was Simple and Direct" by Dean Hughes and Tom Hughes, from *We'll Bring the World His Truth: Missionary Adventures from Around the World* (Salt Lake City: Deseret Book Company, 1995), p. 23.

"To My Missionary Son" by Gay N. Blanchard, from Barbara B. Smith and Shirley W. Thomas, comp., *Where Feelings Flower* (Salt Lake City: Bookcraft, 1992), p. 140.

"The Golden Contact" by Kevin Stoker, from *Missionary Moments* (Salt Lake City: Bookcraft, 1989), pp. 17–18.

"Sanctified by Service" by Carlos E. Asay, from *The Seven M's of Missionary Service* (Salt Lake City: Bookcraft, 1996), pp. 124–25.

"Missionary Miracles" by Mary Ellen Edmunds, from *Love Is a Verb* (Salt Lake City: Deseret Book Company, 1995), pp. 55–56

"The Shoes" by Ardeth Greene Kapp, from *A Perfect Brightness of Hope* (Salt Lake City: Deseret Book Company, 1997), pp. 60–61.